THE PASTOR'S NOTEBOOK

The Pastor's Notebook

JOHN HUGHES

To Richard & Lisa

May God richly bless you in this
new phase. May he bring into
being what is not.

much love

John.

1 John 2.27
2 Sam 7.3.

KINGSWAY PUBLICATIONS
EASTBOURNE

ISBN 1 84291 043 4

Published by
KINGSWAY COMMUNICATIONS LTD
Lottbridge Drove, Eastbourne BN23 6NT, England.
Email: books@kingsway.co.uk

Book design and production for the publishers by
Bookprint Creative Services, P.O. Box 827, BN21 3YJ, England.
Printed in Great Britain.

This book is dedicated to Anne, my wife and companion on the journey and an instinctive pastor, and to my three sons, Tim, Peter and Stephen, whose hunger for God has been an encouragement and an inspiration.

Contents

Foreword

In my own ministry of oversight as a bishop, I am acutely aware of the pressures, challenges and opportunities faced by all who are in pastoral ministry and leadership. We live within a materialistic, fast-changing and fragile society in which many people feel that the care and support they need at times of crisis are either unavailable or insufficient. Pastors themselves can sometimes feel overwhelmed and ill-equipped to respond, even insecure in their own identity as men and women called by God to a ministry of pastoral care and Christian leadership. Yet, at the same time, the opportunities to be channels of the compassion and transforming love of Christ to others are often, quite literally, right there on our doorstep.

Then there is the wrestling with the searching questions of how to reshape the church for its mission so that it is more in touch with the local community and contemporary society.

- What pattern of services do we need?
- How can we make our church building more wel-

coming and adaptable to serve the needs of the local
community?

- How can the gifts and ministries of the whole people
  of God be maximized?
- What about pressing financial matters?
- How can prayer be given a greater priority?

These and many more issues are all part of an ongoing
process that requires vision, courage and wisdom in
leadership, arising out of prayerful discernment of the
mind of Christ and the leading of the Holy Spirit.

This is why *The Pastor's Notebook* is so welcome and
timely. It comes not from someone who claims to be an
expert, but from a pastor and leader with over 34 years
of pastoral ministry under his belt, who is prepared to
share his own vulnerability and failures, as well as his
strengths and achievements. That's why Canon John
Hughes' notebook has such an authentic ring about it
from start to finish. This is why the reader can identify
with so much that is generously and honestly shared.
His warning that 'one of the surest ways to kill the spiritual life is on the altar of busyness, where we are driven,
not by the Lord, but by the pressures of society', is one
of the uncomfortable, but highly necessary, strands running through his notebook. Too often we are driven by
'musts'.

Throughout, John Hughes calls upon the rich resources of the Scriptures for inspiration and illustration,
as well as from the writings of others whose expertise in
various pastoral disciplines has played its part in the
formation and development of his own pastoral ministry. It was said of a certain missionary that 'he walks
as he talks'. His life was all of one piece. As a colleague

of John's in the early stages of his ministry, I can say of him 'he walks as he writes'. In turn, in the last chapter he takes as his supreme pastoral model Jesus Christ the Good Shepherd, commending him afresh to all his readers.

The Pastor's Notebook will, I believe, be an invaluable resource to all who seek to grow in their understanding of how to be more effective in their pastoral care and leadership. It is a worthy edition to this fine series of 'Notebooks'.

The Right Reverend John Perry
Bishop of Chelmsford

Introduction:
The Journey of a Pastor

As an introduction to *The Pastor's Notebook*, I thought it might be helpful to trace something of my journey as a pastor and reflect on what I have learnt and what has been passed on to me by others over 34 years of pastoral ministry.

I have had the privilege of serving in four parishes in different dioceses and have visited many other parishes to speak on renewal, growth, faith, unlocking churches from the past, and the healing ministry. This has usually been with a team from the parish, so that it remains credible because we are illustrating the learning process of our journey of faith. Concrete examples are helpful to others, not as a blueprint to follow, but as a source of principles that may serve to guide them on their journey. I hope that this book may be helpful to pastors leading different churches, illustrating our need to hear constantly what God is saying and to step forward in faith to do his bidding. The secret of movement is that we look to the Lord of the church for his purpose and seek to do what he says. That is to build on a secure and lasting foundation.

> Therefore everyone who hears these words of mine and puts them into practice is like a wise man who built his house on the rock. The rain came down, the streams rose, the winds blew and beat against that house; yet it did not fall, because it had its foundation on the rock. (Matthew 7:24–25)

The pastor's primary role is to lead the church in that walk of faith and obedience.

I served a title for four years at St Andrew's Church, Chorleywood, under the vicar John Perry, who went on to become Warden of Lee Abbey, Bishop of Southampton and Bishop of Chelmsford. St Andrew's was a daughter church to Christchurch, Chorleywood. It became an ecclesiastical district then a parish church, and over 30 or more years has grown considerably as a centre of leadership, training and renewal under John Perry, David Pytches and latterly Mark Stibbe. Chorleywood is a wealthy suburban town with private and council housing, a prime commuter area for London. The rich resources of leadership, creative thinking and ability in the community have been harnessed to make St Andrew's a growing church.

John was a marvellous pastor and visionary leader with an ability to delegate, inspire and grow new leaders. During my time there, St Andrew's was a growing church that was discovering the new life of the Holy Spirit, which John and his wife Gay experienced at Lee Abbey. John came back to share what he had discovered, and the people were open to risk and followed him with a vision and heart to move forward with God. They completed building a new church and launched it with a mission to the parish involving Harry Sutton, the

General Secretary of SAMS (South American Missionary Society). It was an exciting place to be. When my four years were up, I was followed by Barry Kissell, a gifted evangelist who was later to lead teams from the parish in a faith-sharing ministry for some 25 years.[1]

In 1971 I moved on to St Stephen's Church in East Twickenham to serve a second curacy with Martin Peppiatt. I was there for five and a half years. This was a church that had known a significant ministry to the community in the war years, under the Revd Russell White, later to be Bishop of Tonbridge. Martin came to the church in 1969. By then the church had a faithful core, but was declining. Over the next 25 years Martin and his wife Cynthia were to see renewal taking hold of the church and bringing remarkable growth and expansion. This was the fulfilment of a wonderful promise given to us at our first staff prayers on Friday the 24th September 1971. Our reading was from the book of Haggai. The church looked back to the war years as its high-water mark, but God was saying to us,

'I will fill this house with glory,' says the LORD Almighty . . . The glory of this present house will be greater than the glory of the former house,' says the LORD Almighty. 'And in this place I will grant peace,' declares the LORD Almighty. (Haggai 2:7b, 9)

Martin had a great pastoral gift. He was also a superb Bible teacher and a man of prayer. I learned a great deal from Martin and Cynthia about steadfast prayer, love,

---

1 Faith Sharing Ministries (FSM) was started in 1974 and has visited 1,000 churches in 23 nations.

patient teaching and encouragement and taking up the cross and following Jesus, in the path of both suffering and glory.

Both curacies gave me an invaluable learning platform in preparation for the two parishes I was to go to serve as vicar. I had been privileged to work with two men with differing gifts and to have two models of leadership from which to learn, as well as experiencing two churches at different phases of development. This gave me a very rich resource for the years ahead. I owe a huge debt of gratitude to John and Gay, and to Martin and Cynthia, whose continuing encouragement and support have been invaluable over 30 years.

I moved first to St Andrew's, High Wycombe, which was vibrant with new life as well as having an older congregation who had faithfully served the daughter church for many years. It had become a district church and part of a new team ministry. My predecessor Tim Watson had done much groundwork and had drawn many young families into the church, but there was yet to be a marrying of the two groups, who had quite different expectations and objectives.

The second church I went to was St John's, Harborne. Like St Stephen's in East Twickenham, St John's had known a very significant move of the Spirit in the 1970s and had taken that renewal out to many churches in the UK and Scandinavia. The vicar had shown immense courage in pastoring the renewal, paying a considerable cost to see it rooted in the church amidst some fierce opposition. The church had experienced a renewal of worship and praise and had seen many significant healings and considerable growth. It had built up a thriving youth and children's work, which became a feature of

the church's life. Yet after a decade the renewal had
ebbed and there were considerable disappointments
and hurts in the church and among the leaders that had
not been addressed. More of that will emerge later, but I
will say here that I thanked God for what he had
instilled into me in those two curacies over nine years. I
would encourage new leaders not to be in too much of a
hurry to move on to a parish of their own. There is a
great value in being mentored by different leaders, and
it will bear fruit in the years that follow.

Another profound learning experience came from the
seven fruitful years I spent as the Wycombe Hospital
chaplain, when I discovered that so many painful pastoral situations have roots stretching back into
unresolved grief or hurt from childhood. For this reason, I have included in this book several chapters on the
whole experience of ministry to the sick and dying –
covering the issues of facing loss, working through
grief, how a pastor can act as a caring 'technician', and
building a theology of hope.

Before I look at the lessons of the journey I do want to
pay an immense tribute to St Andrew's, High Wycombe,
who stepped out on a journey of adventure and were
willing to take many risks, trusting and proving God's
faithfulness and provision.

I also count it a great privilege to have been Vicar of
St John's, Harbourne. It has been an honour to lead such
a resourceful church, with many gifted leaders and
people. There has been a maturity among its leaders,
who have walked with Christ over many years. That
journey with them has deepened my faith and taught us
to see God's mercy and goodness.

1

The Pastor's Personal Growth

Pastors cannot teach others what they are not learning to live out in their own lives. Their own growth and development is crucial to the growth and development of their ministry and consequently to the growth and the maturity of the church that they lead. So many ministries burn out and falter because this fact has not been seriously addressed. I know it has been my strong desire to run the full course of ministry, not just to have a good beginning and fade out. St Paul spoke about the self-discipline that is needed if we are to run and complete the race. 'No, I beat my body and make it my slave so that after I have preached to others, I myself will not be disqualified for the prize' (1 Corinthians 9:27).

He also writes to the young leader Timothy about keeping his head in all situations. He encourages him to keep going so that he will receive the Lord's award, given on the day when the Lord will appear.

I have fought the good fight, I have finished the race, I have kept the faith. Now there is in store for me the crown of righteousness, which the Lord, the righteous Judge, will

17

award to me on that day – and not only to me, but also to
all who have longed for his appearing. (2 Timothy 4:7–8)

We always need to keep before us God's destiny for our
lives so that we do not jeopardize our calling for the
sake of instant gratification, as Esau risked his birthright
for a 'mess of pottage' (Genesis 25:34).

The courage to learn

One can see from the lives of Saul and David that a
good beginning does not guarantee a good ending. The
difference between the two men was that David had a
teachable spirit, although he made many mistakes,
whereas Saul was so insecure that he was unwilling to
face prophetic correction and thus prevented God's purpose being fulfilled in his and other people's lives.
David learned many hard lessons on his journey that
were to have a profound impact on the lives of everyone
in his kingdom. He could receive prophetic encouragement and correction that shaped the person he was
becoming, whereas Saul could not and therefore had to
be laid aside.

Dr Martyn Lloyd-Jones of Westminster Chapel said,
'The worst thing that can happen to a man is to succeed
before he is ready.' Saul was a case in point. He never
faced up to that inferiority complex, which could not
brook any rival. That was the primary reason for God
rejecting him. I believe that is true of many pastors.
Because of their personal insecurities, they are not able
to delegate authority or hold the reins of leadership
loosely, for fear of what might go wrong. Such attitudes
block the purposes of God's kingdom and contribute to

a dying church. Realizing who we are and what gifts God has given us is crucial to building up and equipping the body of Christ. God's purpose is that the whole body of Christ should be built up until we all reach unity in the faith and in the knowledge of the Son of God and become mature. A one-man band or an insecure leader who blocks the growth and development of others will never contribute to that maturity (Ephesians 4:12–13).

I think this warning is very apposite for a pastor and minister of the gospel. We can do untold damage to the faith of our people if we do not walk carefully and deal with the issues in our own lives that prevent true partnership.

As I will describe in Chapter 8, I was inducted into the parish of St John's, Harborne, on the 17th January 1992, the feast day of St Anthony of Egypt, where I was born. St Anthony heard the call of God to sell what he had, give it to the poor and follow the Lord. In response Anthony went into the desert, where he lived in complete solitude. There he faced the 'wild beasts within', and when he emerged people recognized in him the qualities of a holy man. Many flocked to him for counsel and direction. What St Anthony faced in the desert were the compulsive desires and motivations of his inner self, which he brought before the transforming power of Jesus Christ. It was the gift of solitude that provided the furnace for that transformation. If we do not at some time face our weaknesses and the demons within us, we will have a limited effect in our ministry because we will fail to grow as people.

Awareness of the dangers

It is interesting that in Peter's first sermon following Pentecost he had a very clear image of what salvation was about. 'With many other words he warned them; and he pleaded with them, "Save yourselves from this corrupt generation"' (Acts 2:40). The image of society here is one of a shipwreck, from which each individual needs to jump and swim for his life. Peter was saying that to stay on the ship called the world was to court disaster. Only by believing the message of the gospel and jumping ship would we be saved.

Our society is under the prince of the power of the air and is a dangerous mixture of domination and seduction, which can entangle us and cause us to lose our own souls. Jesus made it clear to his disciples that they must deny themselves, take up their cross and follow him.

> For whoever wants to save his life will lose it, but whoever loses his life for me will find it. What good will it be for a man if he gains the whole world, yet forfeits his own soul? (Matthew 16:25–26)

The basic question we have to face is whether we have been so seduced by the world that we are blind to our own and other people's fate and have lost the power to resist swimming with the tide.

The temptations of the world

One of the surest ways to kill the spiritual life is on the altar of busyness, where we are driven not by the Lord but by the pressures of society. As pastors we have many meetings to attend, visits to make and services to lead. We could have enough activity to fill 24 hours a day and often live life under pressure, becoming so distracted that we do not know how to rest and enjoy moments of space. We are driven by 'musts': we must attract people to church; we must entertain the young people; we must raise money to keep afloat; our community must respect us. This focus, however, addresses the outer façade rather than the inner life. If we look at these compulsions truthfully, we will detect a fear of failure and insecurity about our identity. We have an innate desire to prove ourselves, to be affirmed and therefore acceptable to all.

Yet security is not to be found in these things, but in knowing who we are in God and realizing that we are loved and accepted. Jesus was given this security at his baptism with the Father's witness, 'This is my Son, whom I love; with him I am well pleased' (Matthew 3:17).

In solitude – away from our busyness – we can face the temptations of the world and come to a place where the Lord drives us, not social pressure. Jesus gained such an inner calm through his time of solitude and temptation in the desert. Two temptations common to pastors are anger and greed. Anger may be frozen in the heart, but grudges can so easily be borne against those we serve because of their demands, or because people do not follow us in the way we hope, or because they are critical of what we are trying to do. Anger is a common response to a sense of being deprived. Similarly, when our sense of self-worth depends on what is being said about us, or when our desires are frustrated, or when our sense of self depends on what we can achieve or acquire, then greed quickly flares up when we see someone else achieving or acquiring more. These demons can hide away, but when they flare up they can do incalculable harm to the cause of the gospel.

The example of Jesus

Frank Lake, author of *Clinical Theology*, has a diagram called the 'Dynamic Cycle of Life' that features the life of Christ.[1] It illustrates the dynamic cycle that was integral to the life and person of Jesus and made him a wholesome human being. There were four essential phases in his life cycle that contributed to his human growth and development and enabled him to minister to others. The cycle divides into two parts, 'input' and 'output'. What we have received determines what we are able to give to others. Out of the abundance of the heart the mouth speaks. If we have not received, we will not have much to give. Jesus at his baptism was filled with the Holy Spirit, and after his temptations he returned in the power of the Holy Spirit.

FRANK LAKE'S DYNAMIC CYCLE

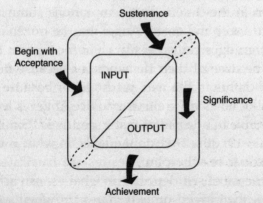

1 Frank Lake, *Clinical Theology* (Darton, Longman & Todd, 1965), p. 133.

Jesus started his ministry from a place of acceptance –
he was not seeking to gain acceptance by what he did. It
began with his baptism by John in the River Jordan. As
he came up out of the water, the Spirit came upon him
as a dove and a voice from heaven affirmed him as
God's Son and assured him of God's pleasure in him.
His Father's delight and pleasure was given for who he
was, not for what he did. He had not yet begun his ministry, yet the Father's pleasure was already expressed
and was not dependent on his success. Those words
were spoken by the Father to nourish and affirm his
Son. They gave him strength and sustenance to go
through temptations, trials, sufferings and rejection and
not cave in.

The second part of the 'input' phase is sustenance.
Jesus gained sustenance from intimacy with his Father,
not from the support of his disciples. At Gethsemane
they could not face what lay ahead and drifted off to
sleep. Angels sent by his Father strengthened him. We
are often trying to travel the other way round: we try to
gain significance from what we do or achieve, and that
never satisfies the human spirit. By contrast, here in this
fierce battle with the enemy, Jesus poured out his heart
to the Father, expressing his fears and feelings. In doing
this he was strengthened for what lay ahead. Thus his
heavenly Father sustained Jesus' life, providing the
resources he needed for ministry. Several times he said
to the disciples, 'I do only what I see the Father doing'
(see John 5:19, 30). That dependence was a powerful
object lesson to his disciples.

Jesus knew that his Father had given him authority
and he used it in keeping with his Father's will. At the
heart of his achievements lay the fact that he lived for

the praise of his Father, not for the plaudits and admiration of the people around him. The need for popular acclaim is something that clearly motivates some politicians, but it can also be a driving force in a pastor's life and we need to be aware of that. Jesus often sought to move away from acclaim and adulation. His achievements and ministry were remarkable, but he worked without stress because he lived a life of dependence on God the Father.

Thus Jesus lived in that dynamic cycle of grace, whereas we often seek to live the other way round and find it exhausting. Sometimes we struggle to achieve acceptance through our success, but this is to travel against the flow. It leaves us drained, because it is a life centred on us rather than focused on the grace of God, which is a gift. Grace reminds us of the empowering presence of God for ministry; it is a channel available to God that he can use. Its focus is not with us. This is a rhythm of life to which we constantly and consciously need to return, because we are raised to be self-sufficient, not interdependent. The struggle of the Galatian Christians was between appreciating life in the Spirit and slipping back into the demands of the Law. 'Are you so foolish? After beginning with the Spirit, are you now trying to attain your goal by human effort?' (Galatians 3:3).

Pressure to 'succeed'

I have been interested to see a sense of exhaustion in many pastors who have been in ministry for more than 25 years. Retirement for them offers the prospect of being able to do the things that really energize them and give sparkle to life. Why does this happen? Why do they no longer find themselves energized by their ministry? There are probably several reasons for this, and they offer food for thought to both pastors and congregations.

We live in a success-orientated society, and this has permeated the church's life. Ministers are judged by what they achieve, by what they deliver. Are they inspiring preachers? Do they pray effectively? Do their prayers heal people? Are they good listeners or counsellors? Are they wise leaders? Do they lead worship in an inspiring and creative way? Are they good at administration and well organized? Are they warm-hearted, caring people, and do their families offer a good example to all? There are so many categories of demands that no one person could begin to meet them all – but each member of the congregation has his or her own categories and the leader is scored against them.

Such demands create pressure and often lead to unhappiness or a sense in the leader that he or she is not coming up to scratch. The inner drive is to work harder and try to cover up these deficiencies. Such an attempt is doomed to failure, however, because the workload is infinite and that course of action will only lead to burnout and depression, as well as depriving spouse and family of the energy, fun and love that is their right. Subconsciously, if not consciously, the pastor also knows that this is not the right way to live, and remains unsatisfied.

The radical response to this problem is to question the expectations and realize that only a corporate solution will lead to a sensible and healthy conclusion. The answer lies in a communal understanding of what 'the body of Christ' is, not in a worldview that is contrary to God's created order. God's creation pattern holds both work and rest in a creative tension. Both are necessary to healthy living.

The church is not a collection of individuals, banging against each other like billiard balls and moving off on their separate ways. Rather, it is a body made up of different parts, where each part is attached to the whole and works for the common good. No one person has all the gifts. Completeness is found only in a healthy interdependence of the whole body.

This means that the church looks to the head, which is Christ, and seeks to recognize the different gifts that are given in his body, discerning where each plays their full part. Maturity only comes when each limb or organ – each person – is playing his or her part in the whole. The responsibility should not fall to the few, but the whole body should take the strain – discerning what it is that each leader brings and understanding how we, the body, can complement and fulfil what is lacking. Such an attitude would eliminate unsustainable pressure and provide a model of life sustainable for both the pastor and the church, creating the right environment for growth and replenishment. The key is to ensure that people are involved in doing a number of jobs that energize and refresh them, instead of doing too many tasks that sap their energy.

The responsibility of leadership is to grow churches that work from this perspective, challenging many modern-day assumptions that are both unhealthy and unworkable. It also counterattacks the modern attitude of consumerism, where people come expecting to receive but have little concept of the part they can play in giving to their community. Health comes from a balanced interplay between giving and receiving. A Christian who comes only to take will be a drain on any church. We need to teach this clearly, so that all Christians might grow as they learn to minister the gifts that God has given them. If God's people learn to act in this way, the leader will not constantly be trying to push an immovable object, but can seek to co-ordinate and encourage the communal initiatives to which God is giving birth.

There is a wonderful story of a vicar who was observed to go to the railway bridge in his parish each afternoon to watch the London train go through. When he was asked why he went each day, he answered, 'I have come to see one of the only things that moves in this parish that I don't have to push.' We need to work towards every member fulfilling his or her God-given calling. Where a church has such a vision and people are trained and supported in the task, that church will thrive and grow.

Money, sex and power

I mention later in the book that the principal temptations today involve money, sex and power. Money manifests itself as power; sex is often used to acquire both money and power; and power is often called 'the best aphrodisiac'. Historically, it is also true that spiritual revivals have been accompanied by a clear, bold response to the issues of money, sex and power, bringing about a strong renewal of devotional and ethical life. Money is such a crucial issue today because we live on credit, and many people are stressed out because they are living wildly beyond their means. Keith Tondeur's work for Credit Action[2] shows how much debt is an issue in modern life, and Christians are by no means exempt from this pressure to conform. A society that is judged on what we acquire and possess and driven by pressure to acquire more is a very dangerous society in which to live.

Today it is all too easy to get into debt. Banks and building societies offer generous loans. Consumer goods come with interest-free credit. We are tempted to measure our worth by what we own. These pressures can be devastating, especially on marriages. The growth of the divorce rate matches the growth of debt. Over 70 per cent of divorced couples state that financial problems were the primary cause of their split. Many sacrifices are made by pastors, and one of them is to forgo a reasonable income – but living in a society that pursues such materialistic objectives can make it hard to be content. The pursuit of riches was one of the temptations Jesus faced.

> The devil took him to a very high mountain and showed him all the kingdoms of the world and their splendour. 'All this I will give you,' he said, 'if you will bow down and worship me.' Jesus said to him, 'Away from me, Satan! For it is written: "Worship the Lord your God, and serve him only."' (Matthew 4:8–10)

So many in society are giving all their energy to acquiring

---

2   Keith Tondeur is director of Credit Action, based in Cambridge, UK. He has written the following useful books: *Your Money or Your Life* (Triangle, 1996), *Financial Tips for the Family* (Hodder & Stoughton, 1997), and with Larry Burkett, *Debt-Free Living* (Monarch, 1997).

money, but they are not living a life. They have no time
for family or relationships, for themselves or for rest, so
they live on the edge of great stress. Jesus recognized
where this was coming from and had the inner strength
to resist it. That strength came from solitude, when he
made the time to reflect and see what was going on
inside him.

Sadly, a number of those in ministry have misused
money or have not learnt how to handle it. I know of
one ordinand who had a problem with money and, in
order to sustain his consuming lifestyle, borrowed over
£30,000 over a period of years from a trusting parish-
ioner and had no means of paying it back. That
ordinand was ordained and served his title. He had an
affair that broke up his marriage, so he moved to
another diocese. It was there that the money problems
surfaced, as he had no way of repaying the loan.
Rightly, that man had to leave the ministry because of
his deception, which should have been spotted much
earlier. Several parishes were negatively affected by his
actions, to say nothing of a marriage and family broken
by the affair and divorce.

It seems that there are many clergy who have had to
leave the ministry following affairs and the break-up of
marriages. These things do not happen suddenly – they
brew up over a period of time. I heard a friend say
something very striking one day: 'It's not how a woman
looks; it's how you look at a woman.' When I was a
curate, a doctor told me, 'Puppy love today leads to a
dog's life tomorrow.'

An affair starts with the eyes, with a look, which
affects the thoughts and leads to action unless it is
resisted. John speaks of this progression: 'For everything

in the world – the cravings of sinful man, the lust of his eyes and the boasting of what he has and does – comes not from the Father but from the world' (1 John 2:16). The same process is recorded in Genesis: 'When the woman saw that the fruit of the tree was good for food and pleasing to the eye, and also desirable for gaining wisdom, she took some and ate it' (Genesis 3:6). The eyes see what is pleasurable, which quickens our desire and motivates us to act, to grasp what is not ours. For this reason the Bible gives the advice that we should watch our looking. Job makes a covenant with his eyes: 'I made a covenant with my eyes not to look lustfully at a girl' (Job 31:1). The psalmist prays, 'Turn my eyes away from worthless things; preserve my life according to your word (Psalm 119:37).

I think that many of the temptations in ministry are appeals to misdirected worship drives. Christians face temptations when the devil assaults them at their point of weakness. We are conditioned by human sin and weakness and a culture that is opposed to the gospel. Succumbing to temptation can quickly bring down the pastor's ministry, and this can become a stumbling-block to many within the church and in the wider community. The number of cases in the papers about paedophile Catholic priests, as well as similar activities by pastors from other traditions, reveals how live an issue holiness – or its lack – is in today's ministry.

Words and deeds

Paul had a great concern for the credibility of the gospel message, and wrote about this in his letters. To the Corinthians he wrote:

Therefore I do not run like a man running aimlessly; I do not fight like a man beating the air. No, I beat my body and make it my slave so that after I have preached to others, I myself will not be disqualified for the prize. (1 Corinthians 9:26–27)

If you preach holiness, you must practise holiness. To the Philippians he said, 'Whatever you have learned or received or heard from me, or seen in me – put it into practice. And the God of peace will be with you' (Philippians 4:9).

Paul boxes with real purpose – he does not hit the air. His aim is self-control, to make his body serve the purposes of the gospel. His goal is self-restraint, not self-flagellation, which he rejects. The bruises he has encountered were hardships suffered for the gospel. He speaks of the self-disciplined journey which is necessary if we are to participate in the promises of the gospel. There is a danger of being 'disqualified', and pastors can do untold damage to the faith of other people if they do not walk carefully and set an example of living in the light. These warnings are real, but he keeps the warning in tension with assurance.

There are two ways in which we can be protected from falling into sin. The first is to be aware of the power of the culture in which we live and to run from temptation if necessary. Paul gives clear advice to the Corinthian church: 'Flee from sexual immorality' (1 Corinthians 6:18); Peter advises, 'Abstain from sinful desires, which war against your soul' (1 Peter 2:11). The second way to protect ourselves is to learn to focus on God through the spiritual disciplines.

Spiritual disciplines

The pastor's personal growth is significant to the growth of the church. It is through the disciplines of listening to God's word, solitude, silence and prayer that we truly face up to what lies within us. All of us are affected by the Fall, and through generational sin and a fallen world carry wounds from our past which affect who we are and how we live in relation to others. To refuse to deal with these issues will circumscribe our potential development and our ability both to relate to others and to welcome the diversity of their gifts. It will also affect our motivation in ministry. It is so easy to be driven by a desire to prove that we can succeed, in order to gain the affirmation or approval we may not have gained from our parents.

Power is also a snare to many in the ministry. It may be used to bolster our self-image. Jesus was tempted to abuse the power that the Father gave to him at his baptism. The temptations were an attempt by Satan to divert the use of God's gifts in an independent way rather than in dependence on the Father's instructions. Thus Satan tempted Jesus with the compulsion of power: 'All this I will give you . . . if you will bow down and worship me.' Jesus said to Satan, 'Away from me, Satan! For it is written: "Worship the Lord your God, and serve him only"' (Matthew 4:9–10).

As we noted earlier, it was in solitude that Jesus found the strength and discernment to recognize Satan's designs and resist them. Solitude gave him the means of seeing – it was where the self was crucified and the struggle was won. Only Christ can overcome this battle against Satan, and only in dependence on him can we too overcome the enemy. Jesus did not overcome by looking at the tempter, but by speaking the word that was in his heart. The battle for victory will be won and the shape of our ministry will be set in times of solitude with God, in times spent 'in the desert'. It is through sacrifice of time with God that we will minister in the power of his Spirit.

The disciplines of silence and prayer are important to the pastor's growth and inner awareness of God at work in his or her life. We live in a world of continuous noise and excessive words. James speaks of taming the tongue:

> Likewise the tongue is a small part of the body, but it makes great boasts. Consider what a great forest is set on fire by a small spark. The tongue also is a fire, a world of evil among the parts of the body. It corrupts the whole person, sets the whole course of his life on fire, and is itself set on fire by hell. (James 3:5–6)

We live in a world of words – so many of them that they often become meaningless. Our words are often unedifying and become weapons that do not reflect the divine word. They do not leave people with a sense of the eternal. How often do you come out of a discussion with a bad taste in your mouth? The writer of the book of Proverbs said, 'When words are many, sin is not absent, but he who holds his tongue is wise' (Proverbs 10:19).

Silence is a discipline, and it gives us time to reflect on the divine word and store it in our heart, until it becomes a fire that burns within us. Sometimes it will mean that our empty words and our fears need to come out in the divine presence and be seen in his light. When he ran from Jezebel, Elijah was asked by God, 'What are you doing here, Elijah?' (1 Kings 19:9). He needed to be able to speak out the threatening words of Jezebel that had pierced his soul and caused him to run for his life. Several times he poured out his fear, and only then did he hear the divine whisper that came out of silence. That word empowered him to go back, fulfil his ministry and mentor his successor Elisha. The Desert Fathers spoke of words as creating communion and life when they embody the silence from which they emerge. Thus Elijah hears the divine, life-giving word when he is before God in silence. That word is the future world breaking into the present.

Our chatty world is full of lifeless words, which have no power to change lives. But silence in which the pastor has heard the word from God and digested it in his or her heart can bring change and transformation, both in the pastor's life and in the life of the people.

The other discipline is prayer, when the pastor stands before God in emptiness and trust. All of us know the importance of prayer, yet it often remains the hardest discipline to achieve in a world of activity. The mind can be a real obstacle to prayer, because prayer asks questions about things that reason cannot fathom. Prayer can also often seem to be like playing a game with God, who appears to be an expert at hide-and-seek.

The writing of the contemplatives has been of great help to many in the nurture of prayer, as they encourage the prayer of the heart. One of the finest formulations of this prayer comes from the Russian mystic Theophan: 'To pray is to descend with the mind into the heart, and there to stand before the face of the Lord, ever-present, all-seeing, within you.'[3]

---

3 Timothy Ware, *The Art of Prayer – An Orthodox Anthology* (Faber & Faber, 1966), p. 110.

Henry Nouen says, 'In the Jewish tradition, "heart" refers to the source of all physical, emotional, intellectual, volitional and moral energies.'[4] It is in the heart that God's Spirit dwells, and there we encounter him. Prayer means coming to the place of truth about what we are and who we are, as well as the truth about God. Prayer is not about many words: a simple word or phrase can help us descend to the heart. A phrase such as 'Jesus, have mercy on me' can help us to enter stillness and to rest where we are in God. The Jesus Prayer – 'Lord Jesus Christ, Son of God, have mercy on me, a sinner' – or some similar phrase can become a way of praying that bypasses the mind and becomes the sound of the heart. It is then that the heart becomes centred on God. Jesus engaged in the regular practice of centring his heart on God, his Father, and that gave him the strength to overcome sin by living a holy life. These disciplines of silence and prayer can keep us from sin and make us aware of the tempter's designs.

A further help in prayer, which Paul mentions in his epistles, is praying with the Spirit, or speaking with tongues. Paul speaks of the benefit of this gift in prayer for personal use, in that it edifies and builds up the speaker. 'He who speaks in a tongue edifies himself . . .' (1 Corinthians 14:4). The gift is edifying because often we do not know how to pray, but in that weakness the Spirit himself intercedes through us with groaning that words cannot express (see Romans 8:26–27). In the Orthodox tradition this groaning is understood as the gift of tears and is primarily a gift of intercession.

This underlines that prayer is more than words; God understands and interprets the message of the heart.

---

4 Henry J. M. Nouen, *The Way of the Heart* (Daybreak, 1981), p. 77.

Often in suffering and pain this is all we can pray. I have certainly found the gift of tongues and the gift of tears an immense help in prayer when my mind has been at a loss for words. God has given us a gift of prayer that can be formulated by the mind or the spirit. It is not a case of 'either, or', but of 'both, and': 'For if I pray in a tongue, my spirit prays, but my mind is unfruitful. So what shall I do? I will pray with my spirit, but I will also pray with my mind' (1 Corinthians 14:14–15).

Practical precautions

The gift can be stirred up at any time and is a valuable weapon to use in times of temptation and in difficult situations where God's wisdom is needed. However, there are other wise precautions that we can take as pastors that will prevent us from running into danger in the first place. This is one of the collects for Morning Prayer:

> O Lord, our heavenly Father, Almighty and everlasting God, who has safely brought us to the beginning of this day; Defend us in the same with thy mighty power; and grant that this day we fall into no sin, neither run into any kind of danger; but that all our doings may be ordered by thy governance, to do always that is righteous in thy sight; through Jesus Christ our Lord. *Amen*.[5]

The following precautions are practical and simple, but are effective safeguards against danger.

The first precaution is not to see a member of the opposite sex for counselling on your own, so that you give no

5 'Third Collect for Grace', Morning Prayer, Book of Common Prayer, 1662.

opportunity for temptation. To make such a habit a pattern of life can save tragedy in later years. So many people have fallen in such circumstances when a habit of discipline could easily have prevented the problem.

It is also good practice to counsel in pairs. This will prevent any danger of dependency on one person, and will offer protection from manipulation and the benefit of increased wisdom. Working in pairs also gives you the ability to hear and observe what is being said as well as reading what is being left unsaid. Moreover, it enables one person to be praying for wisdom and insight and have an ear to hear God, while the other is leading the counselling at that moment. In a church context it is wise not to counsel or pray regularly with a person of the opposite sex, as this can easily lead to a spiritual or emotional attachment.

A further way to avoid temptation is to be accountable to a trusted friend of the same sex, who can challenge you and ask questions freely. Honesty and accountability in peer relationships can help us to grow to maturity in Christ and will help to nip temptations in the bud.

I am part of a cell group that has been a great support whenever pressures in ministry have needed to be faced. We meet twice a year for a couple of days, to share, listen, prophesy and pray for one another. For many of us this has been an invaluable resource through which we have seen God at work transforming situations and bringing new hope. I know this has been an enormous means of mutual encouragement, support and prayer, which has enabled us all to persevere and see situations change over the years.

We need to realize that we are all in a spiritual battle.

Our enemy knows our weaknesses and the strategies he can deploy when we are off guard. To build protection against this is both wise and necessary for the long haul of ministry.

A spiritual director is a helpful guide to a growing spiritual life. So many ministries could be helped to grow to fullness if only we were prepared to accept such a discipline.

These disciplines can help us to run and complete the race to which God has called us. We need to take such practical wisdom seriously, being aware of how much damage can be caused to God's name and to the church by inappropriate behaviour when things go wrong.

My prayer is that we may be able to say with Paul:

> I have fought the good fight, I have finished the race, I have kept the faith. Now there is in store for me the crown of righteousness, which the Lord, the righteous Judge, will award to me on that day – and not only to me, but also to all who have longed for his appearing. (2 Timothy 4:7–8)

2

Leading a Church into Renewal

In January 1977 I left Twickenham, where I had served
my second curacy, to go with my new wife Annie to
lead St Andrew's, High Wycombe. The church was part
of a team ministry set up by the Vicar of High
Wycombe, John Crisp, consisting of six district churches
with their own District Church Councils (DCCs) and a
central Parochial Church Council (PCC).

Phases of growth

It is helpful to know something about the church's history, for that is a very important factor in understanding
its growth and development. We need to know where
we have come from if we are to build a future from the
past. The past gives us important clues about the soul
and psyche of the church and the wisdom to see the
way forward.

St Andrew's Church had three distinct phases in its
development. The first was a decision in 1897 by the
parish church, All Saints, to plant a daughter church
with a Sunday school to serve the community at the east

end of town. This was a bold and visionary step that had a missionary concern primarily to reach children.

The second phase was a decision in 1960 to relocate the church to a new housing estate at the north-east end of town, an expanding industrial area. This represented another courageous step by the church, involving a death and resurrection for the purpose of mission in a newly developing part of the parish.

The third phase came in the 1970s. Previously a curate-in-charge based at the parish church had responsibility for St Andrew's and took an evening service there. The morning service was held in the parish church. The curate would stay for three years and then move on to his own parish. This had two effects: there was inevitably a short-term vision because the curate was never there for long, and the congregation of St Andrew's necessarily took on a significant leadership role. The lay leaders did a wonderful job in maintaining the church through some difficult times, but it was not until the churches in Wycombe formed a team ministry in 1971, with a team vicar providing long-term leadership for each district, that strategy and vision for the church became much more of a reality. (The team was extended in 1975 to include three other churches.) The previous short-term outlook did cause some problems, however. One of these was that the laity had become used to having responsibility for running the church, with the clergy just passing through. The arrival of a vicar with a five-year, renewable contract meant a difficult adjustment for the lay leaders who had previously held the reins of control in their own hands.

Tim Watson was appointed as the first team vicar. Tim was an evangelist and pastor, with a heart to reach out

to the community. One of the central weekly meetings of
the church was called the Friday Fellowship. This had
started as a youth fellowship in the 1920s, with no cut-
off age, and it had gradually become an old-age
fellowship where real care and social support was provided, but little outreach was undertaken. Tim came to
the church, however, because he saw that there were
some couples who were praying for renewal. They
prayed for new couples to join the church, bringing in
experience from outside. He also saw the potential of
the new housing estate with many young families. He
was a decisive leader, with enthusiasm and a warm personality, and he set about introducing new things to the
life of the church. He started a morning family service,
reaching out to those on the estate. Many younger families joined the church through baptism, and soon there
was a steady stream of new Christians being nurtured.
Tim's pioneering helped to build up a church that was
learning to trust God and to give generously, but there
was an ongoing struggle with some members of the old
order, who felt that Tim was disturbing their church.

Handling conflict

In 1977, after six years, Tim left and I came to replace
him. In many ways it was a young church that knew the
gospel but needed teaching and pastoring. Tim had
built a good leadership team, all in their thirties or for-
ties, with some older folk between 55 and 75. The
church had an absence of people of middle age between
45 and 55. In effect there were two congregations, with
very different styles of service in the morning and
evening. The older congregation felt displaced by the

influx of new people, emerging leaders with vision and
enthusiasm. The struggle between old and new was to
be a painful and ongoing one over the next five years.

As a young vicar I found conflict difficult to handle,
and instinctively tried to keep everyone happy. Rather
than addressing the conflict, I carried it within, with the
result that I was pulled in both directions. The focus of
the conflict was the worship, involving the organist and
the choir. I wanted to use the good of both old and new:
'Every teacher of the law who has been instructed about
the kingdom of heaven is like the owner of a house who
brings out of his storeroom new treasures as well as old'
(Matthew 13:52). We had a growing congregation that
appreciated both styles. The organist served both the
morning and evening congregations, but did not like the
modern, less formal style of music we used for the family services. He played the worship songs but was
uncomfortable with them and also found the new
Alternative Service Book liturgy hard to stomach when
it was introduced. He carried his stress quietly, but
many could sense he was not at ease.

The matter came to a crunch at Easter 1982, when he
offered his resignation. I accepted. I thought it right to
close both the morning and evening choirs and to form
one new choir from any who would like to join, to lead
the worship of the church. We had a very accomplished
organist and music teacher who was comfortable with
a breadth of worship styles and had lately been responsible for the morning congregation. Many felt that
this was the right solution, though it was a very painful
step to take.

The image of something dying and something new
coming to birth is a central image of our faith, but that

particular dying brought a lot of pain and anger to the surface. A few left the church saying they could never forgive me for what I had done to their church. If I wanted the Holy Spirit and the healing ministry, they said, why didn't I leave the Church of England and join the Pentecostal Church?

I arranged a meeting with the choir, curate and wardens where the anger and hurt could be expressed and people could speak their minds. It was a very painful process for all of us, but it exposed a possessive attitude to the church. The anger was focused on me, for I had spoilt 'their' church. The issue was one of ownership: to whom did the church belong – the people, the vicar, or God? That repressed anger had surfaced on some previous occasions, when I could feel the resistance, and it certainly polluted the atmosphere. There had been significant growth, but the underlying conflict over worship was hindering the process. The boil had now been lanced, but the wound was painful and I felt responsible. Could I have handled it better? If I had dealt with it differently, would the people have accepted change more easily and not been hurt?

That inner question was answered remarkably when I was speaking at Lee Abbey following the storms in 1983. On a walk in the grounds, I asked the estate manager why the oaks had been uprooted on the escarpment while a row of poplar trees remained standing. The estate manager said instinctively, 'Oh, they could bend with the wind!' I felt God saying to me, 'John, the wind of my Spirit has been blowing, and what cannot yield to it will be uprooted.'

Looking back, that moment was a watershed for me and the church. An important feature of leadership and pastoral ministry is to face and confront issues that hold the church back. Another vital feature is to learn from mistakes. The primary concern of the church was to seek and do the will of God. After that point, the members of the church began to move forward together and growth began to mushroom.

As a pastor, something inside me was broken. I was freed from the fear of people, from the need to try to keep everybody happy. Such an idea was an illusion, for I had been torn in all sorts of directions and had not kept everyone happy. I saw that I had been motivated by a need to be liked and appreciated, but had chosen the wrong way to meet that need. I thank God for that moment, because I saw that the growth of a pastor happens *in the process of* ministry, not before we become ministers. It is crucial that we learn continually from our reactions in the ministry and our attitudes to other people, and that we learn to face up to our weaknesses. We can only lead people where we have learnt to be led.

It reminds me of the marvellous story of an American rancher who held a 21st birthday party for his daughter and welcomed the hundreds of guests to his home. He invited any young man to swim a length of the pool and said he would give that man half his estate or a million dollars, or, he said with a smile on his face, the hand of his daughter in marriage.

They all looked at the pool and saw a shark at the shallow end. Suddenly there was a splash and they saw a young man swimming determinedly for the other end. The rest of the young men cheered and ran for the far end. Fortunately, the shark was soporific and did not immediately waken to the proximity of its prey. The young men pulled the swimmer out just before the shark got to him.

The rancher said to the young man, 'Do you want half my estate?'

'No,' replied the young man.

'Do you want a million dollars?'

'No.'

'Do you want the hand of my daughter in marriage?'

'No.'

'What *do* you want?' said the puzzled rancher finally.

'I want to know who pushed me in.'

I think that is so true of Christian ministry. God intends to push us out of our depth so that we learn to trust him, and so that we see him at work and his kingdom coming.

Building for future ministry

In 1980–83 St Andrew's began to look seriously at building an extension to the church. We had three major reasons. First, we were called to be a 'worshipping community'. The original church was built for 80 people, with an all-purpose hall which could accommodate another 80 or so. The congregation now numbered approximately 270 people, including children, which meant we were bursting at the seams and had no room for further growth. Moreover, the long tunnel shape of the building made participation and hearing difficult. Second, we were called to be a 'witnessing community', which would naturally lead to considerable, ongoing growth. Third, we were called to be a 'serving community'. We had very limited facilities for mothers and toddlers, lunch clubs, and so on – social opportunities that were lacking in the community around us. All these factors pointed to the need for an extension.

When we shared this with the wider church at a special meeting, the news exposed all sorts of fears and a number spoke very strongly against such a proposal. Some believed I was empire-building; some said that an extension was not needed; others asked why we were planning to spend so much money on ourselves when there was such need in the Third World. We realized that we as a council had been living with this possibility for some time, and the people needed time to adjust to the idea. We therefore suggested that everyone should go away and talk about it in their small groups and in twos and threes, and we would hold another meeting after a month.

People need time to take something on board and to speak out their fears in order to face them together. I think some of the older people who had built the new church in the 1960s remembered how much it had taken out of them and felt unable to go through it again. One young man called Mark offered to build a model of the church and the extension from the initial architect's drawings, so that people could see it more clearly.

A month later we had a large meeting at which the model was displayed. The vision for the extension was explained again, and the model showed the kind of facility that would be possible. The model took people's breath away, and many were genuinely enthused about such a possibility. We also spoke about the Third World dilemma, believing that if people really learned to give sacrificially to such a project our general giving would increase considerably, so releasing more funds for overseas. (That proved true. Our giving after the extension rose to over £150,000, whereas before it had been in the region of £30–40,000.) At the meeting we then distributed a form asking two questions, to which the answer was 'Yes' or 'No':

1. Do you feel that God is calling us to build an extension?
2. Would you support it financially and in prayer?

The forms were returned to us over the next two weeks, and the result was that 94 per cent said 'Yes' to building the extension, and 82 per cent said they would support it financially and in prayer. God had turned things round and had shown us how important it was to give people time to express their concerns, to talk things out and to seek God about the plans.

One further watershed moment came during our extension project, on Mothering Sunday, when the children had come in for the last part of the service. We were in the new hall downstairs and the new church was still in the process of being built above us. In a moment of quiet, one lady screamed out in a very disturbing way and another fell to the floor.

I remember my colleague Ian saying, 'It's all right. God is at work.'

I'm glad about that, I thought, but I'd like to know what he's up to! How was I going to explain this to the children? The youngsters were obviously alarmed by what they had seen and heard, and I prayed, 'Help, Lord!' It is the best prayer I know in such circumstances.

I found myself saying, 'Children, what do you do when you're hurt?'

They immediately answered, 'Cry for Mummy.'

'What does Mummy do?' I asked.

'She puts us on her knee and comforts us.'

'Then what happens?'

'When we're all right, we go off and play.'

'That's right,' I said. 'But some children don't have Mummies or Daddies there to comfort them. When they're hurt, they learn to swallow the hurt. They do this every time they get hurt. Now God's church is a family, and I believe that God knew one of his children was hurting and thought this was a safe place for her to find comfort.'

I said to the adults, 'I believe God is asking if he can trust us to look after people who are in pain and bring them his comfort.'

This explanation satisfied the children, and a calm returned to the church. The two ladies were taken out to a different room to be prayed for and counselled. One child said over lunch, 'Mum, isn't it marvellous that Jesus is healing that lady's hurt?' I realized that being pushed outside my experience was uncomfortable and challenging, but God would give me the wisdom to understand and handle what was happening. That was such an important step in being open to the Holy Spirit's moving.

'Let the priests weep'

During the time when the extension was being built, the church sent me on a three-week visit to the Vineyard Church at Anaheim, California, led by John Wimber. I went to an MC-5-10 Conference, a course on the healing ministry that John had first taught at Fuller Seminary College in Pasadena. I had heard him speak at St Andrew's, Chorleywood, when he came over to Britain in 1984 and had been very impressed by his teaching, healing ministry and humility.

That conference was a special turning-point in my ministry. I went longing to receive the power of the Holy Spirit so that I might be more effective in ministry. I did not feel the experience of power that many others did, but I found that I was weeping on every occasion we met for worship. I would start weeping while people from the church would say, 'More, Lord.' I did not understand what was happening, but felt these verses coming to mind: 'Daughters of Jerusalem, do not weep for me; weep for yourselves and for your children' (Luke 23:28), and, 'Let the priests . . . weep between the temple porch and the altar. Let them say, "Spare your people, O LORD"' (Joel 2:17).

I began to sense that I was weeping over two things. The first was personal: I was weeping for myself, God was releasing my hurts and wounds and bringing his comfort to those waste places. Second, God was giving me a burden to weep for others. I remembered a prayer I had made many years before, at a young people's house party, when I read the Joel 2:17 passage and thought, 'I know nothing of what the prophet is describing, but I would love God to give me a sensitive heart that can feel the burdens of others.' I had prayed for that new heart and here, some 16 years later, God was giving it to me (see also Exodus 32:32). Specifically, I was given a burden of intercession for three people I had talked with and counselled on numerous occasions without seeing any resolution in their lives. Day by day I prayed for them and wept for them, in a way that I had never known previously.

When I returned from America I saw each of these

people, and God had done something marvellous in their lives. The first, a dustman called Derek who lived opposite the church, knocked at the vicarage door one evening when I was chairing a DCC meeting. One of the subjects we were looking at was evangelism. Derek asked to see me urgently, and Annie felt it was important enough to disturb the meeting.

When I saw Derek on the doorstep, he said, 'John, I've got news for you. I gave my life to Christ at a Billy Graham satellite relay in High Wycombe. I've nearly done it on several occasions at church, but never had the bottle to go forward. But after Billy Graham spoke, I found myself propelled up to the front. I've had a rough life, but now I feel so clean and happy. I've never felt this happy in all my life.'

I was amazed. Then I found myself saying, 'Derek, we've got a meeting on evangelism in the sitting room. Would you come in and tell those folk your story?'

Derek came in and told them exactly what he had told me, and then he broke down and wept. Through the tears he said, 'I don't know why I'm weeping, because I'm so happy!' He left the DCC stunned by what they had heard. If this is what happens when God gives you the grace of intercession, I thought, we need more of it!

The other two people for whom I had been weeping and praying were women whose spiritual journeys had been arrested in their early years. Margaret could not face Communion and frequently ran out of the church when people were receiving. The next time I saw her, I asked her if anyone had ever cursed her or spoken harsh words over her. 'Yes,' she said. 'When I was a young Christian I joined a church where they were strong on discipleship, and things were asked of me that

I thought were intrusive. I rebelled against their demands and eventually the leader said, "Either you do what we say, or leave the church. If you do that, God's blessing will never be on your life."'

That was a form of curse, and it still lay over her life, however rationally she tried to dismiss it. I saw it as a key to her fear of being near to God – she was afraid that his blessing had been removed from her. I suggested that we pray together, and that she might choose to forgive that pastor, because unforgiveness holds one in bondage to past hurts. Margaret willingly released that person and I, as a pastor, asked God's forgiveness for the abuse we lay on our people. Then I asked God to break the curse. Margaret felt a complete release and was able to take Communion without further difficulty.

It was a salutary reminder that as pastors we need to be careful not to allow personal frustration and anger to cause us to say damaging things over people that can have long-term consequences for their lives. God has given us authority, but such authority can be abused. When we do say harsh things to people, those words come with the power of our office and can be a kind of curse. Just as positive words can bless and encourage, so negative words will harm and discourage. When you see the effect on others, it makes you very aware of the crushing power of negative words and the long-term harm they can cause if not retracted or broken.

The other lady, Jenny, had a fear of large meetings, especially those that were open to the Holy Spirit. She too would sometimes find she could not remain in church. I saw her shortly after my return from America. While I was talking with her, I had an impression that something had happened to her when she was 16. I asked her directly, and she replied, 'Yes. I was at a large meeting in Ireland with adults and young people. The speaker asked the Holy Spirit to come, and many things started to happen which I didn't understand and which made me very afraid. Some people fell to the floor, some spoke in tongues, so I ran out of the meeting.'

I realized that her fearful reaction could have been avoided if the leader had given some explanation of what was taking place, so that those in the meeting would see that he was at peace about it, rather than thinking that things were wildly out of control. I was able to pray over this and release Jenny from that spirit of fear, asking God to go back to that young girl of 16 and fill her with his peace. That prayer was the beginning of a deep work of the Holy Spirit in Jenny. She began to hear God's voice in many exciting and fruitful ways that affected her life, her family and her work.

I also shared with the whole church what God had been saying and doing in me during my visit to America. I had realized deeply that the church belonged to God and that I had sometimes held things too tightly. I asked forgiveness from the church for the times when I had sought to control events out of fear of what might happen, or from fear of being out of my depth and not being able to handle it. The answers to my prayers for Terry, Margaret and Jenny had a profound effect on me, and released a new dimension of the Spirit's work in the church.

Learning to trust God's wisdom

There were two further instances when God led us into the deep end and proved his ability to give wisdom to lead and pastor the church. The first came during the building of the new church extension, a project that was to cost £750,000. The second was an incident at a healing conference in the new church.

We were involved in building the new church at St Andrew's from June 1984 until April 1986. This was an amazing adventure of faith, in which we had to step out and trust God for the finances. The diocese initially said to us that we had to raise 75 per cent of the total cost before we started, which at that stage would have been over £400,000. We said that would be impossible, because this was a faith venture and we were trusting God to provide the means. We had a day of prayer and giving to launch the venture on St Andrew's Day 1983, and raised £17,000 in cash, with further pledges of covenanted giving of £39,700, giving us a total of £66,800 with tax refunds.

Also on that day of prayer, God spoke prophetically to us through a lady called Joyce, who had a vision of the new church. She saw the new church with a lot of glass so that we could see out into the community. She saw people streaming up the hill bringing gifts of all kinds to the church. Inside the church she saw an altar on which there was a burning fire that was consuming the gifts people brought. The fire seemed to have a voracious appetite, and yet the people kept coming with their gifts. Suddenly the fire dropped to a flickering flame. In the flame she could see the new church. Then she saw the words over the church: 'The sacrifice doesn't matter, the building is for the people.'

This picture left us with a sense of awe for several reasons. First, Joyce, who had been a missionary and a matron of a local public school, was not in favour of spending vast sums of money when there was so much need across the world. Second, the picture spoke so much of the sacrifice that would be involved, but emphasized that the primary purpose was for the people of the community St Andrew's was to serve. It also confirmed to us that God was in this step of faith, and it was a marvellous sign that God was going ahead of us.

During the building we faced many challenges – financial, political and physical. One of these physical challenges concerned our chief carpenter, a delightful man called Len. One day, while he was working on joining the roof of the old church to the new extension, he stepped back and fell some 25 feet to the concrete floor. He broke every rib and one leg, and it was feared that he had a clot on the brain from hitting his head on some scaffolding.

We heard nothing about this until the evening, when our architect Alex Roberts told us what had happened. Annie and I were shocked by the news and called our colleague Ian to come up to the vicarage so that we could talk and pray. Later we rang the hospital, to find that Len had been transferred to the Intensive Therapy Unit at the Radcliffe Infirmary in Oxford.

We decided to drive to Oxford and pray for Len. At the hospital we were ushered in to meet Len's wife, who was very shocked and distressed. We talked with her and asked if we could pray for Len. She agreed, and the three of us went into the ITU and prayed over Len, asking God to spare him. We prayed quietly, using the gift of tongues – a very helpful prayer language when we do not know how we ought to pray. We talked with Len's wife for a little while, and prayed for her, and then went home.

The next morning I called nine key leaders together to tell them of what had happened. I said I thought God was calling us to pray along the lines of James 5:14–16. James speaks about calling the elders together and confessing their sins to one another. We split into three groups of three and spent something like an hour in prayer and talk, sharing honestly where our lives were and what our struggles were. It was an incredibly open and transparent time, and brought us very close to one another in our vulnerability. We then met together and prayed for Len with faith, confessing where we had failed God as a church.

What particularly came to mind was how, over the previous five days, I had called the church to prayer in the early morning and later in the evening because God had spoken to me from Nehemiah 4:9 when I had been praying over some of the difficulties of the building: 'But we prayed to our God and posted a guard day and night to meet this threat.' A number of people had come to pray, but I distinctly felt that God had been warning us of danger and we had not taken it seriously and were therefore vulnerable to Satan's designs. 'Put on the full armour of God so that you can take your stand against the devil's schemes' (Ephesians 5:11).

At the Sunday morning service the next day, I shared this news with the church. I went on to say that if Len were to die, I would feel no joy in the completion of the new church, only sadness. I said that I felt we needed to ask God's mercy, because I believed he had warned us to pray and we had not been alert to that. I felt some blame and wanted to ask God's forgiveness.

Someone shouted out, 'John, it's not your fault!'

I replied, 'I believe when we hear God's voice there is

a greater responsibility upon us to obey.'

I led the church in prayers of repentance, and we were taken into a very profound time of repentance and asking God for his mercy of healing. God spoke to us some words of prophecy and comfort, and we felt I should return to the hospital to pray, taking with me a lady called Carol who had a vision of Len on the ITU bed being healed.

Carol and I drove to the Radcliffe Infirmary, and we prayed over Len. I found myself talking to him of the Good Shepherd who left the 99 that were safe and went after the one who was hurting. I bent down and said to Len, 'Len, I sense you are disorientated and hurting, but Jesus the Good Shepherd is coming to where you are and he is carrying you to safety.'

As I said these words, Len opened his eyes, sat up and said to me, 'Is the roof covered?'

'Yes, Len, it is covered,' I replied.

I turned to the nurses and told them Len had spoken and was sitting up. They quickly came and injected him so that he went to sleep. I felt such praise to God, for I saw it as a sign that Len's mind was okay and he was going to get better.

Len came out of hospital three weeks later and came to church the next Sunday. I was not there, but the church that had wept in prayer now cheered to the rafters. It was a very remarkable healing and left us with a sense of awe and a realization that if God said things to us we needed to take heed of them and act accordingly. We had been privileged to see God's future kingdom breaking into the present.

Fear transformed

A further occasion when a difficult situation was transformed came at a healing conference held at St
Andrew's in 1986, led by a Vineyard team from
America. They had been with John Wimber at a
Westminster Conference in London, and came to us for
the weekend. We had some 400 people with us for that
occasion. On the first evening of the conference a young
Vineyard pastor called Randy was speaking. At the conclusion of his talk, a lady stood up and screamed from
the front row, 'My husband is dead!' He had slid off his
chair and collapsed to the floor. A feeling of icy fear covered the church. I looked at Randy and saw that his jaw
had dropped. Fortunately, two doctors ran to the front
and began to resuscitate the man, while an ambulance
was called.

I went up to the front and said to Randy, 'May I say
something?' Then I asked the church to sit down and
said, 'I know there is great fear in the church at what we
have seen. I believe this is a spiritual attack, because if
this man were to have died none of us would want to be
engaged in the healing ministry. I would like to pray.'

I prayed that God would break the power of fear in
the church and banish any work of darkness that was
opposed to his kingdom. I prayed for the man,
Malcolm, who had collapsed. A calm and peace came
over the church while the ambulance men took Malcolm
out on a stretcher and rushed him off to hospital.

What came out of that evening in terms of praying for
people was remarkable. There were several in the
church who struggled with a wish to commit suicide.
When they saw the anguish of the woman over her

husband, they realized the anguish they caused to their own partners. One was a mother suffering from post-natal depression. As we prayed for her, she renounced her death-wish in Jesus' name, and we prayed that in Jesus' name the power of that death-wish would be broken. Then we prayed for the peace of God to fill her and heal the wounds. She felt a great peace and lightness in her heart. God certainly healed that mother, for she went on to have more children and never suffered from any further depression.

At the end of that evening's ministry we were worn out, but really thankful that God had been at work and had turned something potentially damaging to good. God does give wisdom to handle his work when it is needed; we simply have to learn to risk and trust him.

When I went the next day to visit Malcolm, the hospital had taken extensive tests and said that he was okay. However, a heart murmur that had been present from childhood was nowhere to be seen on the X-rays, so he felt that God had been at work in his life in a special way. He was sent home that day and wondered whether he should come to the church in the evening. I suggested that he might be better off having a rest, but promised that I would pass on his greeting to the church.

Renewal takes place when we have the courage to respond to God's agenda and are willing to be on the cutting edge. A new phase of growth came through building the church extension that effectively tripled our size and gave us a wonderful building to use. That journey of faith profoundly affected the whole congregation, in experiencing God's miraculous provision, in discovering the power of prayer, and in sharing what we were discovering with the wider community. Thus evangelism was happening in the workplace. It was not a case of 'we ought to share our faith with others', but rather, 'we cannot *but* speak of the things we have seen and heard'.[1]

A fruit of that faith project was that we learned to give sacrificially and to release resources of people, finance and talents. Teams have gone out from St Andrew's to share lessons of faith, renewal and witness. The income that was £1,000 in 1970 reached £168,000 in 1991, with over a third given away outside the parish.

Principles for renewal

Looking back on those years, some important principles emerged as crucial features for the renewal of the church.[2]

1. The growth of a church is cyclical; it involves an ebb and flow. The ebb often provides a time of questioning and reflection where God calls his people to listen afresh to him and face up to unaddressed issues. The journey of Israel in the Old Testament provides a remarkable illustration of this pattern. The phases of advance were often preceded by times of desolation,[3] which provided an impetus to seek God anew.

---

1 *Bucks Free Press* articles, December 1984. From December 1984 until April 1986, when the building was completed, the local paper carried a number of articles about this adventure of faith, which was a talking-point in the town.
2 See David Gillett and Michael Scott-Joynt, *Treasures in the Field* (Fount, 1993), pp. 58–61.
3 See Gerard W. Hughes, *The God of Surprises* (Darton, Longman and Todd, 1985), p. 96.

2. Growth in the church is dependent on the growth of the leader. Leaders can often block growth and renewal through their own personal fears and insecurities. This prevents lay participation, because such people are often perceived as a threat. God needs to deal with these issues in a leader, for that leader's capacity for growth is vital to the growth of the church. I found this was critical to the release of St Andrew's. When I visited the Vineyard Church in America, God touched and broke me over insecurities which had resulted in holding the reins of the church too tightly and fearing to let go fully and trust God. This led to a new depth of trust and a willingness to step out beyond my own comfort zones and those of the church. It ushered in a new experience of God's presence and provision. It reminded me of a truth of leadership: that a church cannot go beyond its leader. To facilitate change, a leader needs to be changing. Peter Senge says, 'To grasp the meaning of "metanoia" is to grasp the deeper meaning of learning, for learning involves a fundamental shift or movement of mind.'[4]

3. Having a vision and communicating the vision are also vital when it comes to encouraging a church to own that vision and bring it into reality. 'Write down the revelation and make it plain on tablets so that a herald may run with it' (Habakkuk 2:2). Clarity of communication is the means of inspiring people to support a vision, thereby bringing it into reality.

---

4   Peter Senge, *Fifth Discipline* (Century Business, 1990), p. 13.

4. Conflict has to be seen as a stepping-stone to growth. It is also part of the process of maturing leadership. The issue of ownership and letting God be Lord of the church is a key to continuing renewal. Renewal seems to ebb when we step back from the cutting edge for a variety of reasons. This principle might be an interpretative key to where renewal fades.

5. The courage to risk failure is the nature of faith. Nothing worthwhile will ever be gained by living within our comfort zone or keeping everyone happy. Successful visions are the fruit of risk. Dr Martin Stephen, headmaster of Manchester Grammar School, once said, 'The greatest hazard in life is to risk nothing.' Such vulnerability in the leadership provides a safe place for people's personal growth. A success culture undermines people's ability to take risks.

6. Learning to see people with faith is also important in order to release the gifts of God in his people. With encouragement, ordinary people can step out to do extraordinary things. In taking teams away to share what God had been doing, we saw people growing in their ability to witness and to pray for others. Many would never have believed they could do such a thing, but now had confidence to witness and pray for people in the workplace and elsewhere.

7. Continuity of leadership is another important factor if a church is to grow beyond the ceiling of about 250 and into the thousands. The church needs to know its Shepherd's voice, and the development of that kind of trust takes time. A leader needs to be committed to the long haul.

These principles were fundamental in the renewal of St Andrew's Church, and have an application to any leaders guiding a church into renewal. We have had the privilege of sharing what we learned with other churches stepping out in faith to build something new. We have felt the honour of 'passing on the baton', in the same way that other churches helped us.[5]

5 See also Michael Baughen, *Moses and the Venture of Faith* (Mowbrays, 1978); Robert Warren, *In the Crucible: The Testing and Growth of a Local Church* (Highland Books, 1989).

3

Ministry to the Sick and Dying

As a curate I visited many hospitals and prayed for the sick and dying on many occasions, but the seven years I spent as a hospital chaplain were extraordinarily enriching. I led a team ministering to both staff and patients in the hospital, and it gave me an insight as a pastor into the National Health Service and a greater understanding of those who work to administrate and to serve in caring for the sick.

In the Wycombe Team Ministry, each district church had a sector ministry, ranging from chaplain to the Church of England school to chaplain to the General Hospital. The role of hospital chaplain was assigned to St Andrew's Church, so I inherited the job from my predecessor, Tim Watson. The hospital had 300 beds, an Accident and Emergency Unit, an Intensive Therapy Unit and a Special Care Baby Unit.

Initially my brief was to visit patients in the hospital and to take Communion round all the wards on a Wednesday morning. It was not long, however, before I realized that the staff were also a priority. They had many pressures to contend with and were clearly in need of support. I therefore started to train a group of laypeople to visit the wards, with volunteers from different churches. This gave me more time to offer support to the staff on the wards and in the various special units. As I built up a relationship with them, they started to talk more openly, and even began to call me in emergencies. I gave particular energy and time to the crisis units.

My experiences as a hospital chaplain taught me to recognize the importance of affirming and encouraging those who are working at the sharp end of life. It is vital that we give time to support them. These people carry considerable burdens and suffer from grief and a variety of other difficult emotions as they work to support patients and families. They are often exposed to anger and abuse, as patients and their families project their own distress onto the staff. The increase of litigation to which doctors, surgeons and hospitals are now subjected is one factor that often militates against the hospital being a healing environment.

I would particularly like to record here a number of experiences that taught me a great deal about understanding and standing with those who were facing death and reactions to that process. I used to visit the A & E Unit regularly, and was also called in to support staff and family members when a child or partner died suddenly.

The gift of time

I was called in once when a little boy called Andrew had been found face down in his neighbours' fish pond. Andrew was 18 months old, the same age as my son

Timothy at that time. He had beautiful blond hair. The attempts to resuscitate him were useless and the team had to admit there was nothing more they could do. The consultant and senior sister brought the parents into the resuscitation room, where they were able to hold their little boy and talk and cry. Both parents spent more than half an hour talking with us and cuddling Andrew, and we gave them time to take in the reality of his sudden death. I know that the gift of time and support they had from the hospital team meant a great deal to them, and it allowed the staff to grieve too.

Such an incident highlights the fact that grief is not simply personal but corporate. It affects not only the family but the community as well – including the hospital staff, and the neighbours in whose pond the boy drowned. There were also issues of blame – or perceived blame – which needed to be worked through. Who left the door open? In this case the door had needed repair because it did not shut properly, but it had not been fixed. If such matters are not brought into the open, they can drive a wedge between family members and cause long-term damage. Feelings of guilt are often there too, and need to be released and healed. Mistakes are part of being human and sometimes have very cruel consequences that no one could foresee. Blame is a form of denial that needs gentleness and time if those involved are to come to terms with the reality that a child has died.

One another occasion I took my new curate, Ian, on a visit to the hospital. It was his first day in the job after being ordained. When we entered A & E the consultant said, 'John, we were just going to ring you. We have a young lady in the rest room whose husband has killed himself in the park, and we're waiting for the under-takers to bring the body in. She's denying it's her husband. Could you go in and see her?'

I went to introduce Ian and myself to the young lady, who was called Katherine. She said she did not know where her husband John was, but his car had been found in the park with a body inside. She was sure it was someone else and John would turn up. I knew it was important to allow her time, because her denial that the body was John was a sign that she could not yet accept the truth.

I asked her about John, and she told me they had been living together for two years and had got married only a fortnight before. She was 18; he was 24. They lived in a caravan and had just come back from honeymoon. She showed me some photos and spoke of the kind of things they enjoyed doing together. John was a very creative person who struggled at times with depression – but it could not be him in the car, she said, because he had set off that day in a good mood.

She kept coming back to this point, and every time I reflected her statement back to her: 'You don't think it's John? You think it's someone else?' Gradually, she became less certain, and eventually admitted that it could be John. Denial is a kind of anaesthetic that numbs the pain. It is, if you like, nature's way of giving a person time to come to a place of realization. As pastors we need to allow people that time: to tear away such a denial with a statement of bald fact is to damage the process of com-ing to terms with the loss, and is not helpful. So, we sat and talked, and in time Katherine began to say that she thought the dead man was her husband, although she had no idea why he might have killed himself.

Her father-in-law came in and sat next to her. He was somewhat abrupt and wanted to get away from the hospital as soon as possible. Katherine said she wanted to see the body when it arrived. Her father-in-law said no: he would confirm it was John, and Katherine should go home in a taxi.

I could feel the atmosphere changing and asked if I could have a word with her father-in-law outside. I suggested that he should allow Katherine to decide what she wanted to do, because if he pressurized her she would feel cheated out of her wishes and would feel antagonistic towards him afterwards. I said that if he let her make the decision about when to leave, he would never regret it.

Back in the rest room, Katherine confirmed that she wanted to see John, so we accompanied her to the mortuary chapel where his body had been taken. The A & E sister came with us. Katherine fainted for a moment when she caught sight of the body, so we took her quickly out. As soon as she could, however, she wanted to go back into the chapel. She talked to John and stroked his hair, cutting off a few locks to keep. She spent quite some time with him, then said she was ready to go, and kissed him.

Over the next few days she returned to A & E and showed the staff photographs from her honeymoon. She obviously felt it was a special place and felt supported and affirmed there. My curate Ian's first visit to the hospital had been quite a baptism of fire, but it showed just how important it is to give people time to make their own journey. In such situations, each person has a unique journey to make.

Individual journeys

I remember being called in one day to see a ward sister's twin baby boys. Both were premature, but one was critically ill with respiratory problems. That child died, leaving the parents struggling to come to terms with what had happened. They needed to grieve the loss of the twin who had died, while coping simultaneously with the baby who had survived. All too easily, their friends focused on the living child, failing to give them permission or space to grieve for the child who had died. I visited the family regularly over some time. Rosemary had a real faith, but her husband Derek found it difficult to believe, because he had been wrongly pressurized as a young boy and felt abused by that experience.

Some six months later, I had a phone call from Rosemary. Derek had been diagnosed with inoperable cancer and had just months to live. She asked if I would visit him, recognizing that he did not want any unwelcome pressure. Derek's illness was a staggering blow to them, especially so soon after the death of their twin baby.

I went regularly to see Derek. He talked at length about the way he had been pressurized as a young boy by keen Christians at school. He felt sickened and put off by that experience and, though he had met Christians he respected, his wife included, he was very wary of their intentions. I remember saying that I thought his word 'sickened' was entirely appropriate; he was quite right in his reaction to vomit it out. I apologized that sometimes as Christians we pressure people in our evangelistic zeal, in a way that robs them of their space and integrity of decision. Derek was very involved in giving to the community and ran a flourishing Cub group. He was a kind and thoughtful man, very supportive of his wife and family. He espoused Christian values even though he was wary of the church.

We also spoke about Derek's reaction to his illness. He was philosophical, thoughtful and lacking in any bitterness. As time went on, he appreciated my praying for him and his family, and later was happy for me to pray for him at his hospital bed. Late one evening I popped in to see him after I had been involved in a training course for hospital visitors. Rosemary was there with him. He was in a coma and clearly near to death. I talked and prayed with Rosemary and said I would return in the morning.

Annie and I prayed for the family as we went to bed that night. The next morning Annie said she had dreamt that Derek had died, but he had said to her quite clearly, 'Please tell John it's all right.' When I rang the hospital, they told me that Derek had died at around 4 a.m. Some time later, I talked with Rosemary and felt it was right to tell her about that dream. She was reassured to hear about it and found it very comforting.

An aside on dreams

Dreams are often experienced at a time of loss or when we are under pressure. They pick up thoughts and feelings which are unresolved. They provide an opportunity to get in touch with what is going on inside, and can bring a resolution to what is disturbing.[1]

---

1 Russ Parker, *Healing Dreams* (SPCK, 1988) is a helpful study on the power and purpose of dreams.

I remember hearing people speak of dreams earlier in my ministry and being somewhat suspicious of the reliance placed on them. I now realize, however, that God often speaks through dreams and visions. One basic conclusion we can draw from the Bible is that dreams are a normal experience of life and, like any other normal experience, can be a vehicle through which God speaks to us. Herman Riffel has observed, 'If we add together all references to dreams and visions and all the stories surrounding them, we would find a third of the Bible is related to the subject.'[2]

The Hebrew word for dream is *harlam*, meaning 'to make whole or healthy'. From dreams we can learn something about our situation and do something about it. We should not be surprised if the God who made and created us can speak to us in dreams and minister his comfort and presence through them.

Family bereavement

On another occasion I was called in after the sudden death of a man with a young family. Edwin and Susan were happily married with two children, Rachel and Simon, and another baby on the way. Edwin went out to play badminton one evening, and within twenty minutes of his return home he died of a heart attack. He was in great agony and died before a doctor could reach him. His death was a terrible shock to the family. Less than four weeks later, Susan gave birth to the baby, Jeremy.

---

2 Herman Riffel, *Your Dreams: God's Neglected Gift* (Kingsway, 1984), p. 24.

Family, friends and members of her local church gave Susan all the help they could. Her father, who had lost his wife from a heart attack the previous year, came to live with the family. Susan coped amazingly well, but the real shock hit her when she returned home after Jeremy's birth. She loved the baby, but felt she was denied time to grieve for her husband because of the baby's needs. She was open with the children about Edwin, however, and they were able to laugh and cry together, sharing their many happy memories. When I visited, I found we could all talk about him very naturally, because he was part of their everyday conversation.

In the early days Susan went often to Edwin's grave. She found strength in these visits, but never admitted to feelings of great anger or bitterness. She did say that she wept every night before going to sleep and that she would then feel a great peace come over her. She felt this was God comforting her, assuring her that Edwin was well. She was also glad to have seen Edwin's body at the undertakers, for he had seemed to be at peace and there was a smile on his face. This relieved her of the memory of his awful death.

Susan's relationship with her children was very good. She set them free to talk about their dad, but they noticed that she was often upset when they did so. Because of this, they did not necessarily share their deepest feelings with her. Rachel was very practical and loved being a mother figure to the new baby, and she seemed to adjust better to the loss. She was outgoing and did well in her schoolwork. She liked to visit her father's grave and insisted on going on her birthday in order to share that day with her father.

Simon's reactions were very different. He became insecure and sometimes emotionally unstable, and had difficulties in settling down to work at school. He developed a particular dislike of going to the church where his father was buried, saying it gave him 'the creeps'. He had not grasped the significance of death as a permanent state, and seemed to feel that his father might reappear. The graveyard was a terrible place to visit, he felt – a place where something awful might happen.

It is important that as pastors we recognize the place of children in grief and seek ways to give them space to talk and so work through their loss. An adult who is close to the children may be in a good place to facilitate this process – but family members and medical staff often have their own grief and reactions to contend with. So often the children's needs can be overlooked because they seem to cope with life as it happens, and more attention tends to be paid to the adult who has lost a partner. If the children are not cared for and supported, however, they will carry that unresolved loss into adult life. This might affect the relationships they form, damaging their capacity to trust themselves to their spouses. For this reason I would like to look more closely at caring for the whole family unit, with a view to supporting all members in the grief process.

Children's reaction to loss

A death in the family is a frightening and unnerving experience for a child. Handled wrongly, it can lead to problems later in life, and even to psychotic disorders (psychosis is a severe form of mental illness that affects the whole personality, and it can be linked to a fear of death or separation as a result of unresolved grief). This is less likely to happen if children are helped to understand their loss and express their grief. Dr Dora Black, a consultant child psychiatrist, has commented, 'Although the adult instinct is to protect a child, the truth, in manageable doses, is the wisest course.'[3]

Adults often assume that children have no capacity for grief. 'Of course, he/she can't understand,' they say. It is true that very young children have no ability to comprehend the meaning of death, since they have no sense of time and space, but it is this very inability that may make their response to acute loss all the more devastating. Children have a sense of omnipotence and feel that all of life is an extension of their own being. They feel secure in the framework of strong arms and loving tenderness. When this is suddenly withdrawn, their security is shattered. Children communicate through emotions before they develop the ability to use language, so while we should not expect them to express grief in an adult way, they still have a need to make a response. If they are helped to express their grief in an appropriate way, the risk of a later depressive illness is lessened. The conspiracy of silence can be bewildering and frightening.

Young children's concept of death is an incomplete and confused one. Before the age of four they cannot understand that death is final, irreversible and occurs to everyone; they need special help in grasping that a dead person cannot move, think, speak, hear or see. They also need to understand that the dead person did not choose to die, and did not die as a result of someone wishing it

---

3 Cruse Lecture at Royal Free Hospital, Hampstead, 1980.

or feeling hostile. Young children think magically and live in a fantasy world. They may also cover up for many years feelings of guilt about the death of a parent or sibling, because they may once have wished that person dead. Simon's father Edwin, for example, died of a heart attack. When Simon was asked if he knew what that meant, he said, 'Soldiers attacked his heart.' He felt that he was somehow guilty of attacking his dad's heart, and was fearful that his dad would retaliate. That was the fear he had whenever he went to the graveyard. He was afraid that his dad might suddenly return and surprise him.

Between the ages of four and seven, children's understanding changes. They are by now busy exploring their world. They are curious about their body and other people's bodies. They will investigate with interest the body of a dead bird. They will try to discover the difference between death and life, asking such questions as, 'Do dead people eat?' 'How do you go to the bathroom when you're dead?' 'Will Granny hear me if I shout very loud?'

From eight to eleven children are seeking to make sense of life, and this is the time when they realize that they must learn to be careful for their own life. They wonder why and how death is experienced in life. They can perhaps understand why old people die, but why young people too? During this time they will also grasp the fact that death is not reversible. They need honesty and sensitivity to help them discover and understand the world in which they live.

Teenagers move into an abstract world – they are capable of grappling with concepts and ideas and not just with the things they see around them. They may want to talk about death or fears of death. They may wish to prove they are not afraid, and may even risk their life to allay such fears. It is important to help teenagers to develop a healthy and positive attitude towards life and death.

Young children cannot remain sad for very long, and their cheerful play can seem very callous to a grieving parent. Adults need help in understanding this difference between their children's emotional world and their own. For instance, a mother could not understand why her daughter did not cry at her father's death, but did so profusely when they had to leave their house. The child could not mourn for something she did not know – i.e. death – but could mourn when she left a home full of love, security and memories. Children under four years of age feel insecure when their relationships have been dislocated. They feel a sense of abandonment. They need to have constant, tender love, which makes them feel secure.

What should children be told when a parent dies?

Religious ideas can be meaningless to families who have no idea of God. In fact, to present the idea of 'heaven' or 'God taking Daddy away' can be very unhelpful to a young child. It would be better to talk about death as the end of life, or about Dad having an illness which the doctors could not make better, unlike many illnesses which they can cure. It is important to allay the fears of death hurting, and equally to prevent the opposite extreme, where the child goes looking for it. One little boy was asked why he had tried to kill himself by putting a plastic bag over his head. 'I wanted to go to be with Daddy,' he replied.

The most helpful thing is to ask the child what he or she feels, and gently put right any misconceptions. It can be helpful to introduce God as someone who is now looking after the person who is dead. Children also need to be told about the grief of the surviving parent, which will gradually get better. They need to be told that it is *not* their job to look after Mummy or Daddy, as other adults will support them.

Should children go to funerals?

Older children and adolescents can be told what goes on and encouraged to go to the funeral if they wish to. Young children might be afraid of returning to church after a funeral, or may pick up a death anxiety, and should be free not to go. If young children do attend the funeral, they should be able to get out at any time, and should have an adult with them for support, preferably one not too closely involved who can provide undivided attention. John E. Schowalter says, 'It is unusual for children under the age of six or seven to experience funerals as a useful event psychologically.'[4] It will be easier if children have previously attended the funeral of a more distant relative or family friend.

How can we help children mourn?

Children might find it hard to talk in adult terms, but might easily talk while doing something with an adult like drawing or modelling. Children should be encouraged to talk about their feelings and their memories. Ask them to show a photograph of the person who has died, and give them permission to be sad or angry at

---

4 *Journal of Pediatrics* Vol. 89 No 1, pp. 139–142.

their loss. Children need to know that they are safe to share their feelings with an adult and that they will not be deserted in their sorrow. Death is an experience of desertion by a loved one, so they easily fear it might happen again.

Preparation for death

Dr Dora Black has said, 'We do not do enough to familiarize children with death.'[5] Keeping pets with a short lifespan is an excellent way of experiencing a manageable bereavement. A pet's death can be mourned, and the animal should have a funeral. Even a lost toy can be an opportunity for a child to learn how to release grief.

I remember when our youngest son Stephen's pet hamster died, leaving him heartbroken. He wrote a letter to Hobby saying how much he loved him and looked forward to seeing him in heaven. It was very moving as he laid that letter in the little grave we had dug. I had just come back from taking a funeral at church, so Stephen wanted me to stay robed and to say some prayers. Our other son Tim and a friend called Ben were watching and trying to contain their mirth, while for Stephen it was deadly serious – he wanted it done properly.

It may not be wise to replace the pet or toy immediately, for that could deny the grieving and healing process. We need to show children how to take advantage of the sorrows in life as a strengthening of character and preparation for a final bereavement. Teachers should also be encouraged to do projects on death and

---

5   Cruse Lecture at Royal Free Hospital, Hampstead, 1980.

so familiarize children with this unavoidable experience of life.[6]

Mourning a stillbirth

Moving on from helping children to cope with death, I would like to focus on one particularly difficult problem for adults. Mourning a stillbirth or a late miscarriage has to be one of the hardest experiences we can face. With about one stillbirth occurring in every eighty deliveries, it is a relatively common tragedy. Yet it is an event which is often cloaked in secrecy and which, by its very nature, seems somehow unreal. Medical practice has often been to remove the evidence as quickly as possible, but this can badly hinder the parents' mourning and healing process.

The difficulty is that after a stillbirth there is no tangible person to mourn. Stillbirth has been described as a 'non-event' in which there is misery, guilt and shame. Often in such cases there is a conspiracy of silence, which only isolates the mother and increases her sense of guilt for having 'failed' as a woman.

Dr Emmanuel Lewis suggests that parents need something tangible in order to mourn.[7] Memory facilitates mourning. He encourages bereaved parents to look at or touch their baby. It helps to name the child so that he or she is integrated into the family, to take part in the certification of the stillbirth, and to have a memorable funeral.

---

6 An excellent book on the subject is E. A. Grollman's *Explaining Death to Children* (Beacon Press, 1967), and another very helpful source is *Death and Family* by Lily Pincus (Faber & Faber, 1976).

7 Emmanuel Lewis, 'Management of Stillbirth', *The Lancet* 18th September 1976, p. 619.

It used to be standard practice for a hospital to hand over the stillbirth to a funeral contractor and for the body to be buried in an unmarked grave. Now hospitals encourage the family to attend a burial or cremation, thus helping them to mourn that reality. A photograph of the child, using some drapes if necessary to hide a deformity, can also be helpful in assuring the family of the baby's reality. It can also help to explain what has happened to any children involved. In my experience, this advice has proved helpful in the mourning process.

Marilyn and David had two stillbirths before it was discovered that Marilyn suffered from placenta deficiency. She saw the first baby by accident and found it possible to accept that loss. But, she said, 'I never saw the second baby and, do you know, it haunts me to this day.'

Another couple, Peter and Melanie, had two girls called Sarah and Penny and were looking forward to the birth of their next child. Melanie had high blood pressure and was admitted to hospital, where the foetal heart stopped. The baby was delivered and they cuddled the beautiful girl for about an hour. Later Peter took a photograph.

When I talked with them and asked them about their child, they both described her features and Melanie cried. I mentioned the value of giving the child a name and holding a funeral service, so this was arranged. Two days later I noticed that the fact was announced in the births column of the *Telegraph*. They also showed the photograph to their two girls, explaining to them what had happened. In this way the family were able to integrate this sadness into their lives and to work through it together.

Understanding and permitting different reactions

Adults express their grief in a variety of ways, and such differences need to be understood. Sometimes one partner may feel that the other is not expressing grief and is bottling it up. Often there can be considerable tensions between a husband and wife mourning the loss of a child, because they do not appreciate the different expressions of emotion that are appropriate for them as individuals.

Timothy and Jenny were expecting their second child some six years after the birth of their son David. His had been a very difficult birth and he had been an active baby, sleeping very little in the first three years. Although Jenny's pregnancy progressed well this time, at full term the foetal heart stopped. The baby was born the next day, beautifully formed, but dead. Both mother and father saw the baby.

Jenny felt very angry and bitter. Three months into the pregnancy she had dreamt that the baby would not live, but had not shared this with anyone. Yet she blamed the doctors for allowing it to happen. Timothy was worried about Jenny's bitterness and wanted to push it away. He did not understand her feelings or her denial of the death. This may have been because he was afraid that he could not handle such strong emotions. He wanted Jenny to accept what had taken place and get on with living. Jenny was aggrieved because she felt that Timothy was too calm. He did not show any grief.

When I talked with them together, it transpired that Timothy had been very seriously ill with asthma during his childhood. This experience had taught him to accept suffering and to live within its restrictions. Jenny needed to understand this means of resolving his struggle with loss of health. He felt no bitterness about the baby's death. In fact, the way Timothy released his grief was not by talking but by going for a walk and playing the electronic organ at home. Jenny had not realized this and felt that he must express his grief as she did. Both needed to allow one another space to express their grief in the appropriate way for themselves. When they did so, they found that they were complementary to each other, and the tensions which had arisen from their misunderstanding were resolved.

At Wycombe Hospital we set up a remembrance book made from beautiful bound leather with loose-leaf parchment pages inside. The name of each child who died was inscribed on a page, which was then painted with flowers by an artist at our church. The book stayed in the chapel, so that parents visiting the hospital could come to the chapel and remember their child. We also had a nurse who specialized in the after-care of parents who had suffered a neonatal death. The hospital held an annual service in church for the parents, and a great number of people came each year. They appreciated seeing the supporting staff, and valued the comfort that the service gave in helping them to own their loss and make the journey forward.

A little child's response sums up beautifully the main message of this chapter: 'When my Daddy was driving we saw a fox lying in the road and nobody stopped. You should always stop and say goodbye to dead things.'

4

The Way to Adaptation and Change

Bereavement is the response to the loss of a beloved person or object. Such a loss is a catastrophic experience and calls for change in the lifestyle of the bereaved, in which they have to give up the assumptions which have guided their life and behaviour, and develop fresh ones which fit the new reality.

Our model for life

Each of us has a model or belief system about life and the world in which we live. This model comprises our individual view of reality as we believe it to be – a strongly held set of assumptions about the world and the self which is confidently maintained and used as a means of recognizing, planning and acting. It might include, for instance, the assumption that when I sit on a chair it will support me; when I go home my wife will be there; when I get up I can stand and walk about. Assumptions such as these are learned and confirmed by the experience of many years. They help me to make correct predictions about the world, and to live and act accordingly.

Sometimes these assumptions are proved wrong. My chair collapses; my wife is out; I trip and fall over. Such accidents may produce a temporary feeling of anger or frustration, but they do not require me to change my pattern of life – only to have the chair repaired; to await my wife's return; to fix the carpet. Just occasionally, however, a life event can bring about a major change, within a short space of time, which renders obsolete a large part of my assumptive world: my wife is not at home because she has died; I fall over when I get out of bed because my leg has been amputated. Events such as these render useless my established set of assumptions, and these must be changed if I am to function normally.

Different people face such catastrophes in different ways. Lily came into hospital for the treatment of an ulcerated leg and finished up by having to undergo an amputation. She could not accept that loss and dared not face the future. The result was that she spent over a year in hospital, for the most part opting out. In contrast, George cut his foot severely on glass. Gangrene set in, resulting in amputation. He accepted and faced that reality, and looked forward to seeing how he could tackle the obstacles ahead. As a result, he healed remarkably quickly and concentrated on adjusting to his new circumstances. His next challenge was to learn how to drive.

Psychologists call an event of this type a 'psychosocial transition'. The old world model cannot fit reality and a new model has to be constructed. The necessary revisions of model are not always easy to achieve. Usually they are completed but only slowly, often they are done imperfectly, and sometimes not done at all. Colin Murray Parkes says,

Such events are not always or necessarily deleterious in their effects and it is often the case that the completion of a successful psycho-social transition leaves the individual stronger, more mature and better equipped to cope with future transitions should they arrive.[1]

Such an event is a turning-point in life, which for some brings about physical or psychological symptoms, and for others social disorganization and suffering.

The process of recovery

When entering into the experience of being bereaved, it is vital that we understand this adaptation and are sensitive to how we may help a person to accept, adjust and move forward. The process of recovery from a period of mourning or rehabilitation involves the discarding of false expectations and behaviour patterns which may have been appropriate to the individual's former life, and the adoption of new expectations and behaviour patterns which are appropriate to his or her current world. Often people will need help in this process, and this will include listening to where they are and opening up the possibilities of new decisions that can affect their way forward. That process may take a considerable time, because changing the assumptions on which one's life is based is difficult.

Gerry had been gradually losing his sight as a result of a hereditary defect. He trained as a woodwork designer, but found it hard to accept his visual

---

1 C. M. Parkes, *Bereavement: Studies of Grief in Adult Life* (Pelican, 1972).

deterioration and struggled to maintain a job he could not manage. Only as he was encouraged to examine the extent of his incapacity, and to grieve for the world he had to give up, was he prepared to use a cane and take on a more basic job that was within his current sight abilities. In making these changes, he began to achieve reasonable self-reliance and to build a new and worthwhile world in which to live.

The implication of this for any of us who are in a position to give support and guidance is that we need to be prepared to assist the other person to examine his or her assumptions. We need to help that person to clarify the old, known world and the new world in prospect, in order to discover which assumptions can be kept, and which must be changed. This is a painful business, but it can be rewarding as it can noticeably raise the quality of life and morale of the person who is changing.

Using the journey of bereavement, I would now like to look at the need for adaptation and change, and try to clarify how pastors can help people in that process. We need to understand the process, because otherwise we may be contributing to the pain rather than helping a person journey through it to a resolution.

The first point to grasp is that the 'bereavement journey' is not a state but a *process*. Grief is a process of realization, of making real the fact of loss. C. S. Lewis writes,

> I thought I could describe a state; make a map of sorrow. Sorrow, however, turns out to be not a state but a process. There is something new to be chronicled every day. Grief is like a long valley, a winding valley where any bend may reveal a totally new landscape.[2]

---

2 C. S. Lewis, *A Grief Observed* (Faber, 1978), p. 47.

In many ways, grief resembles a physical injury more closely than any other type of illness. The loss may be spoken of as 'a terrible blow', and pain remains while the 'wound' gradually heals. Occasionally the healing of physical injuries is delayed, or a further blow reopens the wound, but normally we expect that process of healing to take place. A similar pattern can be observed in bereavement: there may be obstacles to the process of healing, but we should expect to move towards that goal.

It is important to remember that grief, though it may be regarded as a kind of illness, can also bring strength. Just as a broken bone can end up stronger than an unbroken one, so the experience of grieving can bring strength and maturity to those who have previously been protected from misfortune. Colin Murray Parkes says, 'The pain of grief is just as much a part of life as the joy of love; it is perhaps the price we pay for love, the cost of commitment.'[3]

I believe that the bereavement journey is possible for all and that the end result can be one of growth and maturity. The bereaved person can begin to function fully once again, as one whose life has been deepened and enriched, who has discovered resources and strength which may in turn strengthen others. The words of St Paul in 1 Corinthians 12:26 are true: 'If one part [one member of the body] suffers, every part suffers with it.' Conversely, it is equally true that if one discovers strength and growth, then all are enriched by this discovery.

---

3 Parkes, *Bereavement*, p. 20.

While stating this belief, I would also point out that it is not a shallow experience, summed up by the thoughtless saying 'you'll get over it', or 'time heals'. C. S. Lewis is right when he equates bereavement with an amputation. The amputee will get back his strength and be able to stump about on his wooden leg. He has 'got over it', but he will always be a one-legged man. Healing is coming to terms with that loss, adjusting one's whole way of life and learning, in order to live within a new framework. Lewis says, 'At present I am learning to get about on crutches. Perhaps I shall presently be given a wooden leg. But I shall never be a biped again.'[4]

The stages of grief

In their research into bereavement, psychologists have observed certain stages that seem typical to all loss. These are helpful for a greater understanding of what the bereaved may be experiencing and what support may be given, but they need to be used with caution. We do well to heed the words of the American psychologist A. F. S. Shand: 'The nature of sorrow is so complex, its effects in different characters so various, that it is rare if not impossible for any writer to show an insight into all of them.'[5]

Most psychologists accept that there are three or four basic stages of grief that are typical in every experience of bereavement. Parkes describes these as 'a succession

---

4 Lewis, *A Grief Observed*, p. 43.

5 A. F. S. Shand, *The Foundations of Character* (1914), quoted in J. Bowlby, 'Process of Mourning', *International Journal of Psycho-Analysis*, 42, 1961, p. 323.

of clinical pictures which blend into and replace one another'.[6] He suggests numbness as the first stage, giving place to pining, which is replaced by depression, and it is only after the stage of depression that recovery occurs.

In his book *The Grief Process* Yorick Spiegel takes up the basic outline developed by D. Fulcomer, dividing grief into four states – shock, control, regression and adaptation.[7] Each of these stages has its own characteristics, and there are considerable differences from one person to another regarding both the length and the form of each stage. No person will fit neatly into the model; some may experience two or more stages together, and may even seem to lapse back into an earlier stage. C. S. Lewis describes his own experience:

> Tonight all the hells of young grief have opened again, the mad words, the bitter resentments, the fluttering stomach, the nightmare unreality, the wallowed-in tears. For in grief nothing 'stays put'. One keeps on emerging from a phase but it always recurs. Round and round, everything repeats. Am I going in circles? Or dare I hope I am on a spiral? But if a spiral, am I going up or down it?[8]

In the pages that follow I shall outline the four stages mentioned above, commenting on certain features within those stages and illustrating them from various bereavement stories.

---

6 Parkes, *Bereavement*, p. 21.

7 Yorick Spiegel, *The Grief Process* (Abingdon Press, 1977), p. 60. D. Fulcomer wrote a Ph.D. thesis on 'The Adjustive Behaviour of Some Recently Bereaved Spouses'.

8 Lewis, *A Grief Observed*, p. 46.

1. Shock

The first stage of shock follows immediately after news of death. Comments such as 'I'm stunned' or 'I don't believe it' sum up the inability to comprehend reality. Bad news may create a temporary numbness, because shock is a built-in buffer that helps us to tolerate the crushing news or fearful scenes of death. There is no right way, initially, for us to comprehend totally the loss of a loved one. Shock numbs us and gives us time to get ready for our bereavement journey.

Karen had given birth to a premature baby boy at 26 weeks. There was little hope of survival. All her children had been seriously premature – two girls had survived, but the first boy had died. Now little Jeremy was dying. Karen could not talk, could not cry, and apparently could not feel anything. Her family and nurses were around her, but she seemed to be living in another world.

The stage of shock does not usually last for long – a few hours, or one or two days at most.

2. Control

This stage follows the experience of shock, and tends to last until the funeral. There are two factors involved: the control which the bereaved exercises over him- or herself for the big event, and the control demanded by family and friends to ensure that the funeral is carried out in a 'socially appropriate' way. Every support is given to the bereaved to make things as easy as possible. Meanwhile, the bereaved person often finds that what is happening seems terribly unreal. Sometimes bereaved people may be overprotected by others doing things for them, so that the reality of the situation does not hit them.

Certainly, the bereaved need support, but they should not be excluded from preparations and decisions, as that only exacerbates a de-realization. It can also disable the bereaved in the period after the funeral, when family and friends leave and they find that they are on their own.

3. Regression

It is after the funeral and the departure of family and friends that the bereaved face the real impact of the loss of the deceased. Without doubt, this is the most critical – and necessary – period of the grief process. Here the bereaved face experiences that are not only extremely painful but often appear very frightening. They feel that they have lost control and are in free fall, not knowing what the outcome will be. Now all the emotions are let loose – feelings of anger, bitterness, denial, guilt, loneliness and tears. The breakdown of their own inner world and the fear of total collapse make it necessary for the bereaved to conserve their energy, so as not to follow the deceased into death. We should not be surprised if tension, irritability, withdrawal and neglect of personal appearance are apparent.

Eva was very dependent on Thomas for everything. She was agoraphobic and epileptic, although few people knew that. Thomas was diagnosed with cancer and died just a few months later. Eva fell apart and could not face up to life without him. She could not face the risk of making a new life, of facing her fears and taking up the responsibilities of life. She died within two months of Thomas's death. Because she had been so dependent, she could not survive without Thomas and gave up the will to live.

There are numerous other emotions of regression experienced by the bereaved, and the most common are outlined below.

Anger

Anger is very often associated with grief. It may be direct anger expressed towards the doctors – 'You failed', or the clergy – 'Couldn't you have done something?', or the funeral director – who symbolizes death for the bereaved person. Anger may also be directed toward the deceased – 'Why have you deserted me?'

Such emotions can often also be experienced in losses that do not involve death. Louise gave birth to a baby boy. Her young husband left her immediately, not wanting to face the responsibility of being a father. She felt tremendous anger towards him, and real self-pity at the plight in which she had been left – deprived of love, material goods, husband and father, and of being special to someone. Her husband remarried and had a child with his second wife, which was very painful for Louise. It took seven years for her to accept the past and let it go. Then she could say, 'It doesn't matter any more; it hurts, but it doesn't matter.' She began to sense hope, though she did have one fear: 'If I have no problem, people will stop loving me.' Only as she admitted her anger, faced it, acted it out and abandoned it could she be set free to move forward. Once she had done that, she could see hope for the future, and even the possibility of remarriage.

Guilt

Often a bereaved person will experience overwhelming feelings of guilt and remorse. A partner witnessing the painful suffering of a spouse may wish for that person's death, or, finding the burden of caring too great, may wish for death as a way of release. Others may feel guilt because they believe they did too little to help, and may try to punish themselves or absolve their guilt by holding an elaborate funeral.

June had cared for her ageing husband through some 18 months of trauma. Michael suffered from various illnesses, including cancer of the throat. He had always wanted to die at home and feared hospitals. During the last months, however, he became very sick – she could no longer care for him and was exhausted. The doctor insisted on hospitalization. Michael was confused and fearful, shouting, 'I don't want to die!' June wished it would end. She was faithful in her visits, and one evening stayed until 9 p.m. Two hours later, Michael died. June wanted assurances that she had done the right thing in allowing hospitalization. It was only when I asked if she felt guilty that she poured out her feelings about Michael's fear, how she had wished it would all end, and leaving him to die alone. She found considerable relief in expressing these emotions and accepting her limitations.

A further sign of guilt may be recognized in attempts to idealize the deceased. Elaborate flowers and eulogies may cover up a feeling that the family failed the deceased in some way. This can be evidence that there are unresolved issues, which are causing feelings of guilt. This may be particularly true in cases of unexpected death or suicide. Sensitivity is required to spot the signals suggesting that unresolved feelings of anger, guilt or helplessness are under the surface.

Denial

One of the most common emotions of bereavement is the denial of its reality, the refusal to accept that the death has taken place, or will take place soon. This denial is common both to those who are dying and to the bereaved. The pain of loss is often expressed in pining, a wish for the person who is gone. A pre-occupation with such thoughts can only give pain. Why should a person experience such a useless and unpleasant emotion? An answer to this question offers a key to this whole phase of grief, and much that follows it.

Pining is the subjective and emotional urge to search for a lost object. Murray Parkes suggests that an adult human being shares the same impulse to search that is shown by many species of animal. It may express itself in an impulse to search for the lost person, seeing him or her in the street, or hearing his or her voice. Lorenz has described the effects of separating a greylag goose from its mate:

> The first response to the disappearance of the partner consists in the anxious attempt to find him again. The goose moves about restlessly by day and night, flying great distances and visiting places where the partner might be found, uttering all the time the penetrating trisyllabic long-distance call . . . The searching expeditions are extended farther and farther and quite often the searcher itself gets lost, or succumbs to an accident. All the objective

observable characteristics of the goose's behaviour on losing its mate are roughly identical with human grief.[9]

Denial may also be expressed in blaming others. People assume that if they deny the fact of death they will be relieved of the pains of grief. Often the quick funeral is an attempt to deny the reality, but in truth it robs the bereaved of the chance to act out their grief.

I met Irene in the psychiatric ward and listened to her story. She was 18 when her father, to whom she was extremely close, committed suicide. He shot himself at home, while his wife and family were downstairs. Irene said her father had been very depressed, had a bad relationship with his wife, and suffered from diabetes. She could not understand why he had committed suicide, however, and was hurt by her mother's explanations – 'Your b***** father shot himself.'

There was an unhealthy silence in the family over the suicide, and all of them struggled in that silence. At the funeral Irene became hysterical and did not go into the crematorium. She felt guilty about 'letting' her father die, and said she often saw him around the place. She was agoraphobic and depressed, and unable to let go of her father. Not long afterwards, her grandparents both died, but she refused to attend their funerals. She became fearful of the death of her husband and young son, and said, 'Fear is my constant companion.'

The refusal to face the reality of her father's suicide and her own feelings of guilt prevented Irene from moving forward and locked her up in the cycle of death. The

---

9 K. Lorenz (1963), quoted in Colin Murray Parkes, *Bereavement* (Tavistock, 1972), p. 58.

refusal of the ritual may have robbed her of permission to grieve and break her denial.

The sense of the deceased's presence can be an attempt to mitigate the harsh reality of death. The basic requirement for working through problems of grief, however, is to deal with the reality as fully and quickly as possible. There is no beneficial therapy in creating a world of falsehoods and dishonest denials. As quickly as the bereaved can marshal their resources, they should face honestly the pain of their deepest feelings and express them with openness and sincerity. As soon as is reasonable, they should also be encouraged to be open and responsive to the feelings of others, for many people will share in their bereavement. Finally, as soon as possible, they should confront the task of reordering their life, assessing their needs and the resources available to meet those needs.

Irene had a confused sense of responsibility, thinking she should have been able to do something to prevent her father's suicide from happening. Such people need a good listener who can help them to distinguish between their own responsibility and the responsibility borne by the deceased. Professional or pastoral help is vital in helping them to make that distinction.

Loneliness

Loneliness is one of the most poignant forms of human suffering, and does not only occur in the bereaved. It is a desperate feeling of separation from those who give meaning to life. It may be the loneliness of the single person who would dearly love to be married, to be special to someone. I have an identical twin brother who, when I got married in 1975, felt an acute sense of loneliness. Others may experience the loneliness of being emotionally shut off from others, unable to make any meaningful human relationships.

The bereaved often face acute loneliness, which is partly the loss of themselves in the deceased. Edgar Jackson describes grief as 'a deep type of loneliness; the bereaved person is longing for the part of himself that he gave in love to another'.[10] One bereaved wife tried to mitigate that loneliness by asserting that her husband had been reincarnated in the house furniture. Her husband had worked in a local furniture business and had made the table that stood in her dining room. She was convinced he was there.

Ultimately, such attempts to cover or deny loneliness are not going to be very helpful. Loneliness is the verification of an empty spot in life that has been left by someone's death. It is a fact that verifies the reality of love. Yet our life does not end with the death of another, and our capacity to love does not end with the loss of the object of our love. The capacity for love remains, waiting for a chance to express itself anew in ways that can enrich life once again. As the bereaved are willing to accept love, so they can learn that even devastating circumstances can open doors to new meaning and new love.

I have summarized above some of the characteristics of regressive behaviour which are often little understood by those supporting the bereaved. I believe that an awareness of these characteristics can help us to listen

---

10 Edgar N. Jackson, *The Many Faces of Grief* (SCM Press, 1977), p. 33.

more effectively and support more constructively those who are making a bereavement journey.

Yorick Spiegel suggests that the process of regression has a particular function in the mourning process:

> Regression can be both the reaction to a traumatic event as well as a mechanism to cope with this experience. While the psychic organization regresses to a simpler form in which the loss still may be mastered, it creates at the same time a starting-point from which to build up new relationships. In this sense regression can be considered a defence mechanism.[11]

In addition to the characteristics described above, an attitude of helplessness may also be displayed. Helplessness is a sign that the bereaved has lost control, but it is also an appeal for comfort and support. Sickness may be another way in which the bereaved expresses a wish to die like the person they have lost, but at the same time it offers relief from daily tasks, and perhaps necessitates care and support from someone else. This enables the bereaved to concentrate their energies on coping with their loss and regaining their balance. It is a necessary part of the process, for only as the bereaved can dissociate from the deceased and let go can they begin to emerge and function in the real world. Thus they make their way forward to the adaptive stage.

4. Adaptation

The final stage of grief is reached as the loss is recognized in full and accepted. In the normal grief process,

---

11 Spiegel, *The Grief Process*, p. 78.

the bereaved not only restore the deceased person within themselves, but also renew their internal world, which has been broken. The restoring of the person within describes a healthy integration of memories and experiences that enrich our lives but do not prevent us from moving forward into a new future.

That experience of 'spring', bringing a new sense of energy and hope, has been described in this way:

> I cannot remember the day when I felt for the first time that not everything is irretrievably lost. One day I noticed that I had ceased to be a façade. I exist to breathe. I wanted again to have influence over events.[12]

This process of adapting is not a continuous one, but often runs back and forth with reminders such as a birthday, anniversary, or particular association with a date, place or event. The effort to deny the loss in the regressive stage and to find the dead person in memories, or to hold on to the past, can bring a greater estrangement than a deliberate willingness to let go. Paradoxically, it is exactly this release and liberation that keeps the lost person present. C. S. Lewis vividly describes this realization:

> Looking back, I see that only a very little time ago I was greatly concerned about my memory of H. and how false it might become. For some reason – the merciful good sense of God is the only one I can think of – I have stopped bothering about that. And the remarkable thing is that since I stopped bothering about it, she seems to meet me every-

---

12 *Ibid.*, p. 82.

where. Meet is far too strong a word. I don't mean anything remotely like an apparition or a voice. I don't mean
even any strikingly emotional experience at any particular
moment. Rather, a sort of unobtrusive but massive sense
that she is just as much as ever a fact to be taken into
account.[13]

It is vital to help the bereaved to release their grief, and
to provide a structure for working out that grief. People
need help to accept the reality of death, to express any
negative feelings, including ambivalence and guilt, and
lastly to incorporate the deceased into themselves. Only
when the lost person has been internalized and becomes
an enriching part of the bereaved is the mourning
process complete, and a place reached where adjustment to the new life can be made successfully. To reach
this place, the bereaved need the structures of ritual that
society provides, and the support of caring people to
help them act out their grief. It is this twofold need that
we will examine in the next chapter – the function of
ritual in grief, and the role of the caring professions.

13 Lewis, *A Grief Observed*, p. 41.

5

The Pastor as a Ritual Care Technician

Today's society badly needs to restore the practice of rituals to help it make sense of and give meaning to the various transitions in life. Rituals are symbolic public acts that recognize the fact of something happening, and that have a symbolic meaning important to the community at large. These transitions have to do with birth, the movement from adolescence to adulthood, marriage, divorce, retirement and death. We might also add to that list, in our complex technological society, the experience of redundancy. Each transition forms a crisis point that needs some form of ritual to acknowledge its reality and to help us move forward.

Rites of passage

These rituals are often expressed in a sacramental form, an outward and visible sign of an inner meaning that marks that particular point of life. The ritual of infant baptism, for example, is the joyful welcoming of a new life, as well as a commitment to helping that child grow up within the framework of the faith, so that he or she might later embrace that faith for him- or herself. It is debatable whether it is the right ritual to be used in a society which has largely abandoned the Christian faith, or whether a service of thanksgiving would be more appropriate. Regardless of that, a ritual of welcome is important to the family, for it acknowledges the reality of the new life and calls them to adjust to the changes it brings.

Adolescence needs a ritual which will help the young person to move from childhood to adulthood, as well as helping parents to acknowledge and accept that transition and reflect it in their attitude and behaviour. The 21st birthday used to be a ritual of such a transition, but the possibility of marriage with parental consent at the age of 16 has made that ceremony redundant. Many young people prefer the age of 18 to mark a rite of passage from childhood to adulthood, as they gain the vote and move on to university, college or work.

The ritual of marriage is important in helping the couple and their families to recognize the new status that has been entered. The marriage service assures the couple of the love and support of the community and their joy in this event, and speaks of its continuity in the birth of future generations. The service helps the parents to 'let go' of the relationship with their children and to allow a new and equal relationship to develop. This service often marks a crisis, especially for mothers, but it is a ritual which helps everyone move forward to a new stage. When that adjustment is not made, many difficulties and tensions can arise. Many young people's dissatisfaction with the civil wedding stems from the reduction of the ritual to a minimum and its resulting sense of anonymity.

The increasing practice of living together without any form of ritual makes it difficult for both family and society to know how to relate to such a union, and to know whether it is permanent or temporary. It certainly offers neither party any sense of security or permanence, and there is no chance to celebrate the relationship. It leaves society with the same sense of uncertainty, and this is not a healthy basis for a growing relationship.

Redundancy has become another crisis transition experience in life, and it seems to be becoming a reality for increasing numbers of people. Being made redundant is a form of bereavement, for it brings a fracturing from society, and creates loss of confidence and self-esteem. Simply to receive a note of dismissal from the employers may seem to add insult to injury: the employee feels aggrieved and the employer escapes from responsibility. To structure some form of ritual of redundancy would allow society, managers and employees to acknowledge an inevitable fact and yet offer tribute and a sense of worth to those being made redundant. This would allow a parting which faces up to the crisis rather than escapes from it. I feel that such a ritual might also give rise to better working relationships between manager and worker, as it would provide a dignified ending, expressing appreciation for work that had been done.

In many firms and the armed services, retirement is often marked by some form of celebration that acknowledges the contribution made by the individual during his or her working life. This ritual both affirms the past and helps the individual move forward to the next stage of life. It is necessary not only for the person retiring, but also for the person taking his or her place, and for workmates who may be worried about the next phase. It gives everyone involved time and space for adjustment and acceptance.

These examples show that the function of ritual is to provide a form for the healthy acting out of transition points in life, making it possible for body, mind and spirit to be engaged simultaneously in actions that give creative direction to living. Rites of passage, rituals and ceremonies not only have their own momentum, but they also tend to move people along in healthy patterns of emotional expression. Anthropologists point out that every culture has surrounded life's crises with forms of ceremony that keep life moving ahead, while at the same time providing opportunities for meaningful physical activity, emotional expression and group support.

Ritual and death

Bereavement is one crisis point in which the place of ritual is vitally important to a healthy mourning process, yet the old patterns of mourning have been almost completely discarded today. Society has increasingly become death-denying, and therefore tends to minimize the rituals surrounding death. 'Please keep it short. I don't know whether I'll cope.' Yet in minimizing death and its rituals, we have also minimized the possible recovery.

In her book *Dying and Creating*[1], Rosemary Gordon has suggested three social phenomena that play a part in this minimization. First, the rapid development of the

---

1 Rosemary Gordon, *Dying and Creating* (Karnac Books, 2000).

physical and biological sciences and the expansion of
technology gave birth to the dream that death could be
conquered, with death often being seen as the result of
medical inefficiency. Second, with the increased mobility and dramatic reduction of the family unit, we are
isolated from death and its mourning rituals. Dying
largely takes place in hospitals these days. Third, there
has been a marked decline in religious traditions and
the belief systems that gave meaning to life and death.

The failure of the dream of conquering death and the
appalling psychological consequences of the denial of
death and loss have led psychologists and anthropologists to favour a proper rite of passage. This gives
people permission and time to grieve, which is far more
therapeutic than the 'mini-funerals' for which modern
Western society, afraid of its feelings, has opted. Twenty
minutes at the crematorium is not sufficient time to
allow a family to acknowledge what has happened.

The trend towards a reduction of the opportunity to
act out deep feelings appears to be a denial of what is
most needed at the time of loss. It is perhaps an extreme
example, but the ceremonial of Queen Elizabeth the
Queen Mother's funeral in the spring of 2002 demon-
strated society's acknowledgement of her death and
was an appropriate and positive rite of passage that
allowed a nation to pay its respects, own its emotions
and move forward.

Philippe Aires has studied the value of life in society
and the impact of death. He comments,

Man's value of life is shown in the practices that are
employed at the time of his death. When life has been
highly valued the funeral process gives significance to the

person who has died, surrounds the ceremonial events with dignity and meaning. When life has lost its social significance, the funeral ceremonies are minimised or eliminated altogether, as with the barbarities of the Nazi prison camps.[2]

The funeral can play a very important part in helping the bereaved to accept their loss. Psychiatrist Dr William Lamers defines the funeral as 'an organized, purposeful, time-limited, flexible group-centered response to death'.

Ritual is there to confront with honesty a painful reality of life. To escape such a confrontation is a form of self-deception that can only complicate the problem of coming to terms with hard facts. The funeral of Diana, Princess of Wales was a case in point. Her sudden and tragic death shook the nation and underlined both our lack of preparedness for death and the fragility of life.

The depth of the outpouring of grief at that time was a result of much more than the emotions associated with the Princess's death: it was also a release of the vast weight of unresolved grief in the nation. The shrines of flowers and books of condolence were important steps for everyone needing to come to terms with the reality of loss. The mammoth ceremonial conveyed that reality to the watching world. The funeral eulogy spoken by her brother, Earl Spencer, was an attempt by him to symbolize her short life and what she meant to so many with all her fragility and brokenness. Her family walking behind the coffin, and the bouquet of flowers with the card saying 'Mummy', were poignant reminders of

2 Cruse lecture at Royal Free Hospital, Hampstead, 1980.

her death at such a young age. The whole occasion, and people's reactions to it, also highlighted how unprepared we are for death and how shocked and rootless we become when we are faced by its sudden intervention.

The ritual of the Princess's funeral, taking some hours to complete, helped a nation to absorb the reality of her death and the idea of a future without her. This is precisely the function of the funeral rite: to confront us with the death of a loved one, and to give us permission to mourn. It is only through that mourning process that separation from the deceased and adaptation to the new situation can be made. The ritual does not replace the grief process, but rather offers an occasion when the community can express their support to those making that journey of bereavement and recovery.

The experience of bereavement is not dissimilar to the experience of a rocket, which is launched into space and has to re-enter the atmosphere precisely through a narrow 're-entry zone'. In bereavement it is vital that re-entry to everyday life is made, otherwise the bereaved will metaphorically be 'flying around in space'. They have to come down to earth. The role of ritual is to help that re-entry to be made.

Meeting the needs of the bereaved

Therapists and psychotherapists would call for the funeral service to be used wisely, to manage the deep feelings of grief. Those who have been working on the re-evaluation of the funeral as a therapeutic resource have defined an eight-step process that is designed to meet the emotional, social, intellectual and spiritual needs of the bereaved. Following those eight steps would make it possible to provide support and comfort, to aid the bereaved in confronting reality, and to create the emotional climate needed to express deep feelings.

1. Verifying the death

The first of these eight steps calls for a verifiable death. It is very hard to begin the process of mourning without verification of the death of the individual who is mourned. Those who lost relatives in wartime – 'missing believed killed' – or those who have experienced a stillbirth or late miscarriage will testify to the truth of that. A viewing of the body can be helpful to the bereaved, especially where there has been a painful death. What is seen is often not nearly as bad as what is imagined.

I remember taking Holy Communion to a ward in the hospital and noticing a lady crying. Her husband had been killed in a car crash in which she had been injured. The Communion service brought up the pain of not having been able to go to his funeral, and the resulting difficulty of realizing his death. I suggested that when she recovered a memorial service might help to meet her need to let go and move forward. She found the suggestion helpful.

In this context it is also important to communicate with all the relatives and friends of the deceased, so that they may be part of the funeral and experience its therapeutic benefits. This process helps in the realization of death and gives a context of support for the relatives and friends. Bereavement never affects only an individual; it also affects the community around that individual.

A funeral service helps to make plain the reality of death. The service eliminates any possibility of denial and can help to start the true work of mourning. My wife's grandmother refused to have a funeral service when her husband died, and afterwards lived to some extent in an idealized and fantasy world. A funeral service helps to set the bereaved on the path they should go. It symbolizes a transition that can help to allay and appease anxieties. It should not be exploited for conversion to faith, but it is an opportunity to put eternal questions before those attending, for they are real questions which they may be facing at such a time.

The funeral service is therefore an aid to a healthy expression of letting go and a conduit for the appropriate expression of emotion, as well as an opportunity to reflect and come to terms with the reality of death. We are celebrating the value of a whole life, not simply its end: the deceased was a person who had relationships with many people and meaning in many lives. The funeral service is an opportunity to give thanks for the meaning of that life.

Pastorally, it is vital to be well informed about the deceased, the quality of his or her relationships, and the dynamics within the family. This will help us to pitch the funeral service in the most appropriate way. It will help to highlight sadnesses or unresolved issues in the family that may need to be owned. If a family row or split has taken place, it may be a regret or sadness that is carried by many. It may be possible somehow to help the family to face that sadness, if they are willing to be open about the situation.

One of the prayers of penitence from the Funeral Service in *Common Worship* may be appropriate for use as a form of confession. This can help a family to acknowledge a reality, let a past problem go and move forward from that event. Truth sets people free, and the acknowledgement of reality allows forgiveness to apply its balm.

> God of mercy,
> we acknowledge that we are all sinners.
> We turn from the wrong that we have thought and
>   said and done,
> and are mindful of all that we have failed to do.
> For the sake of Jesus, who died for us,
> forgive us for all that is past,
> and help us to live each day
> in the light of Christ our Lord.
> Amen.[3]

Where the relationships have been rich and wholesome, it can be helpful for members of the family to take an active part in the service – saying a few words, reading a poem or playing a musical item or song. Some of the most memorable funeral services I have known have included tributes from family or friends, who have spoken very movingly about qualities in the deceased that inspired them. Such opportunities do resonate very deeply, and they can make a service very meaningful for all who attend.

2. Facing sorrow

The second of the eight steps is that we need to face the experience of sorrow and letting go. It may be painful,

---

3 'Funeral Service', *Common Worship – Pastoral Services* (Church House Publishing, 2000), p. 261.

but it is necessary if we are to pick up the pieces and move forward. C. S. Lewis writes superbly on the pain of that journey:

> Do I hope that if feeling disguises itself as thought I shall feel less? Aren't all these notes the senseless writhings of a man who won't accept the fact that there is nothing we can do with suffering except to suffer it?[4]

We cannot prevent the pain by denial; we can only begin the journey through that pain, facing it with honesty and the support of those around us, and eventually coming through to a place of acceptance.

Mary Magdalene's visit to the empty tomb gives us a vivid example of such a journey. She is painfully aware of the death of Jesus. Sleepless, she goes to the tomb to apply the burial preparations, only to find to her horror that the stone has been rolled away. She presumes that the body has been stolen, and runs to find Peter and John. Later Mary stands outside the tomb crying, a natural consequence of loss. Twice she is asked why is she crying, first by the angels and then by Jesus. The reason she gives is that the body has been stolen and she has nothing to mourn. Jesus reveals himself to her by calling her name. She immediately responds and clings on to him, but Jesus says, 'Do not hold on to me, for I have not yet returned to the Father. Go instead to my brothers and tell them, "I am returning to my Father and your Father, to my God and your God"' (see John 20:1–18).

Mary has to let go of Jesus – the separation is necessary. The experience of sorrow is part of the separating

---

4 Lewis, *A Grief Observed*, p. 29.

of identity between the deceased and the bereaved that needs to take place if there is to be a healthy reintegration. The bereavement journey is possible for all if the right support is provided, resulting in greater maturity and the ability of the bereaved person to function fully as someone who is able to live in the present moment.

3. Hope

The third step involved in the funeral service is the offer of hope. Jesus speaks to our innate need of hope for the future. In any funeral service we are confronted with a sense of our own mortality. It is healthy to face that reality. Many people have questions about life and death, even if they do not articulate them. What lies beyond death? Is there such a reality as resurrection?

Paul specifically addresses such questions in 1 Corinthians 15. Some sceptic, he says, is sure to say, 'Show me how resurrection works. Give me a diagram; draw me a picture. What does this resurrection body look like?' Looking for an illustration that will resonate with people's experience of life, Paul sees a parallel in the realm of nature:

> You plant a dead seed; soon there is a flourishing plant. There is no visual likeness between seed and plant. What we plant in the soil and what grows out of it doesn't look anything alike. The dead body we bury in the ground and the resurrection body that comes out of it will be dramatically different.[5]

---

5 Eugene H. Peterson, *The Message* (NavPress, 1995), p. 368; cf. 1 Corinthians 15:38ff., NIV.

What has happened? The seed planted has split apart in the earth and the natural reaction with the soil and water brings about a new body that is different from the body first planted in the soil. This new body has emerged through death.

Paul says that nature is 'a sketch' at best, but it nevertheless helps us in approaching the mystery of resurrection. What he is arguing is that the principle of resurrection seen in nature's cycle is a principle that operates in the spiritual world. That principle is rooted in the death and resurrection of Jesus Christ, who said, 'I am the resurrection and the life. He who believes in me will live, even though he dies; and whoever lives and believes in me will never die. Do you believe this?' (John 11:25–26). The resurrection of Jesus Christ from the dead is the source of hope for us all. Death does not have the final word – life does.

I was brought up as a boy in Simons Town in South Africa, near the Cape of Good Hope. That cape provides a wonderful illustration for death and resurrection. Originally it was called the Cape of the Storms, because it was littered with shipwrecks and many people died there. Then a Portuguese sailor named Vasco da Gama sailed round the Cape to India and returned safely by the same route. The cape was renamed the Cape of Good Hope. No one doubted that a skilled sailor had conquered it. Likewise, before Jesus there was a vague belief in resurrection. The Pharisees certainly believed in it, but the Sadducees did not. Then Jesus conquered death. The substance of resurrection hope rests solely on Jesus, who lived, died, was buried and rose from the dead. This is the hope that over the centuries has given confidence to Christians when facing death. It turns

death from a fear to a hope – in the knowledge that
eternal life is a reality.

Such hope enabled Bishop Brent to write these powerful lines on 'What is Dying?':

> I am standing on the seashore. A ship sails and spreads her
> white sails in the morning breeze and starts for the ocean.
> She is an object of beauty and I stand watching her till at
> last she fades on the horizon, and someone at my side says,
> 'She is gone.'
>
> Gone where?
>
> Gone from my sight, that is all; she is just as large in the
> masts, hulls and spars as she was when I saw her, and just
> as able to bear her load of living freight to its destination.
> The diminished size and total loss of sight is in me, not in
> her, and just at the moment when someone at my side says,
> 'She is gone,' there are others who are watching her com-
> ing, and other voices take up a glad shout, 'There she
> comes!'
>
> That is 'dying'.

4. The supporting community

The fourth step involves the wider community – family
friends, parishioners, colleagues of the bereaved. They
have an important supportive contribution to make as
they share in the attempt to confront the reality, and
thereby confirm it. The love and willingness to stay with
the bereaved can help to create a climate in which real
feelings can be expressed rather than denied. So often
the church or local community can also give practical
help and support by bringing food, or calling in for a
chat once the funeral is over, when the close family support has often moved away.

5. *Spiritual resources*

The fifth step is a focus on the spiritual resources available for moving beyond the past and into the future, where the rest of life must be lived. It can also be an opportunity to confront the reality of death and its meaning for those who are still alive. It is important that the minister releases people to be free to express their emotions and not to be embarrassed by them. As mentioned earlier, the funeral service is a celebration of the whole of life, and needs to resonate with people's memories of the deceased. While the funeral is for those who are still living, it affirms that a life has been lived and valued, and in so doing it enhances all of life.

6. *The disposal of the body*

The sixth step is that the funeral service provides a means for the disposal of the body. The internment completes the process of dealing with the physical aspect of death, but at the same time it verifies the promise of resurrection: as the grain of wheat falls into the ground, it creates the possibility for growth. In many ways, a burial can be more helpful than a cremation in terms of the journey through grief, as one has more time to take in the separation. People can stand around the grave without having to rush on, while there is limited time for this at a crematorium.[6]

I was recently involved with a very moving funeral at the crematorium, which was followed by a thanksgiving

---

6   Of course, in the case of certain illnesses, cremation is a
    requirement, not an option, whatever the preferences of the
    deceased and bereaved might be.

service in church. The couple, Gwen and Michael, had been married for 64 years and had a remarkable relationship that was an inspiration to many. They were very committed Christians. Gwen had been suffering from cancer for some years, and in her last months the family was very open with all who visited, and many were inspired by the way they were all facing the reality of her death. They were helping each other to come to terms with the impending loss. Michael had to face the loss of Gwen and the thought of coping on his own, while Gwen needed to say goodbye to Michael, who would have to fend without her. God was very close to them at that time.

At the crematorium, following the blessing, Michael made his way up to the catafalque, which had not been lowered. He reached out to touch the coffin and then kiss it, as an expression of his final farewell to Gwen. It was very poignant. He had specifically asked that the catafalque should not be lowered at the committal prayer, because he wanted to say goodbye. Sometimes it is worth discussing with the family how they want to handle this, because psychologically it is healthy to be able to choose when you are ready to say goodbye. At a burial you can choose the moment when you leave, whereas at a crematorium the person is often taken from you, and it can feel as if they are being snatched away.

Most funerals do take place at the crematorium, which means that a service in church is eliminated and the whole ceremony is reduced to twenty minutes. Twenty minutes gives little time to face the reality of death and the consequences of grief. If the family is agnostic or atheist, then this situation may be quite appropriate, though ritual still has an important function to fulfil. If the bereaved have some church link, however, they should be encouraged to have a service in church, followed by the short service of committal at the crematorium. A further service of burial of the ashes can take place after the funeral. A marked location provides a place and focus for the bereaved to visit and find comfort later on.

7. An end to the grieving process

The seventh step is to provide some form of ceremonial 're-entry' for the bereaved. The idea of having a memorial service a year later can be helpful in marking the end of the grieving process. The function of such a service could be symbolically to release the dead and to re-enter life.

In my church we arrange a memorial service every year on the nearest Sunday afternoon to All Souls Day. Throughout the year, whenever we take a funeral we invite the bereaved family to come back for that half-hour memorial service. At the beginning of the service the congregation are invited to light one of the small candles set out on tables at the front of the church. The names of all those who have died in the past year are read out from our Remembrance Book. Also included in the service are prayers, readings and hymns. The service draws in a number of people from the community and is deeply appreciated. Afterwards tea and cakes are served in the hall, and there is a chance to talk. As a result, we have had a number of elderly people deciding to come to church, or to attend a group that meets during the week, especially if lifts are available. The service provides a wonderful pastoral opportunity and a bridge to ongoing relationships through our lay pastors or visitors.[7]

8. Pastoral care

The eighth and final step is the provision of adequate pastoral care. The funeral helps the journey of grief to begin, but it is very important to ensure a continuing pastoral care by family, friends and/or the care-giving agencies. It may help the bereaved to visit the church for a service a few weeks after the death. They can also be included in the church's prayers. This used to be a regular practice, and could be revived with value to the whole family of the deceased.

The role of the minister

This leads us quite naturally on to look more closely at the role of those who support the bereaved. Yorick Spiegel describes them as 'care-giving agents' or 'transition technicians'. Those in this role would include the physician, the GP, the funeral director, the minister and the social worker. I particularly want to make some comment on the role of the minister.

Ministers can play a significant part in helping both individuals and society towards a healthier attitude to death. They understand that grief is a process of realizations, of making real the fact of loss. They speak to the

---

7 Lay pastors are a small group in the congregation who possess recognized pastoral gifts and who visit people in need. They meet with the Director of Pastoral Care for training and supervision. In addition, lay visitors make regular visits to the elderly or housebound.

bereaved as people who are aware of their own mortality, for death affects them too. As Bowers says, ministers are vulnerable:

> He/she seeks to represent the divine whilst being human, would seek to give insight into the mysteries that are ultimately as mysterious to him/her as to others. He/she would speak of immortality while deeply aware of his/her own mortality. He/she would seek to explain the meaning of death when he/she has only conjectures and not answers.[8]

To help others, ministers must have resolved their own attitude to death, otherwise they will transfer their own anxiety, or hide from reality behind spiritualized actions and pious words. Their great contribution can be just to be there, listening and helping people to express their feelings of love, hate or anger. Often ministers may be a focus of anger towards God, and it is important to draw out those feelings and not react in self-defence. I have often found that people are greatly helped by being 'given permission' to weep or to feel relief at a death, or even to own their ambivalent feelings towards the deceased. To accept and look at these feelings brings considerable relief and a release of false guilt – and a minister can often be the right person to help with this process.

A visit prior to the funeral can help the minister to assess how the family are coping and interacting with one another, and what anxieties or guilt may be apparent.

---

8 Margaretta Bowers et al, *Counselling the Dying* (Jason Aronson, 1964), p. 63.

This will be useful in making the ritual and funeral address personal and appropriate to helping the family face their loss. Bereavement is never a lone experience; it touches all the family, and it is therefore important to minister to the whole family.

It may be a very positive step if the minister can arrange to meet the whole family prior to the funeral – and so try to help the family work through things together, or give particular help with children, who are often left out or even sent away, which can leave a permanent mark. I remember a person in one of my previous congregations who had a deeply caring nature and was often caring for others. The source of that caring was a desire to rescue those who were hurting, because she had known the hurt of sudden death which had not reached a resolution.

The hospital chaplain

I also think that the hospital chaplain has a very significant role to play as a 'transition technician' in the pastoral care of the sick and ministry to the bereaved. Hospitals are very aware of the inadequacy of this care and the lack of support that sometimes exists. Medical staff also need support and understanding. The denial of death can be very strong in a hospital situation, where it can be seen as 'medical inefficiency', or ignored because the doctor has difficulty in coming to terms with its reality. Many doctors might be motivated to go into medicine in order to overcome their own fears concerning death, and may therefore find it very hard to accept deaths that happen under their care.

In many ways, the role of the priest in society has been taken over by GPs and social workers. They are extremely well trained, but are not equipped to answer the spiritual questions of those who are searching for faith and meaning in the face of a crisis. The chaplain can add a dimension to the total hospital care which is otherwise lacking – standing with the medical team in a crisis unit, taking on the responsibility of caring for the families of the critically ill, or being involved in the diffi-cult decisions that have to be made. Often such responsibility falls on the shoulders of nursing staff, who can feel ill-equipped and burdened by the strain.

The chaplain's additional role of helping the medical and nursing staff in their own attitudes to dying and death can only improve the quality of care. During my time as a hospital chaplain I was involved in setting up a seminar for trainee nurses on the care of the dying. This proved useful in helping them to express their fears and talk through difficult experiences.

Through the link with the hospital social worker, the chaplain is also able to alert the parish priest of bereaved families, especially those at risk, so that the church can truly be a caring community, giving practi-cal help and emotional support. If the chaplain wins the respect of staff, he or she may open their hearts to the role the church can play in society at its different points of need.

Extending our horizons

Before I leave this subject I would like to share the story of a baby boy called Jonathan, whose illness and death had a profound effect on St John's Church and the wider community.

Jonathan's parents, Lionel and Mary, were missionaries

who had returned from Uganda. They had four healthy children, but Jonathan was born severely handicapped. He suffered from neurogenic arthro-gryposis, which meant that some of his muscles and nerves worked and others did not, so he could not control his movements. He also suffered from laryngomalacia, so his airways did not work properly and he needed assistance to breathe – he underwent a tracheotomy to enable him to breathe safely, but was prone to chest infections. He also had some brain damage and was registered blind, just being able to see some light.

Despite his many troubles, Jonathan was a contented little baby and greatly loved by his family and many friends. He loved company and seemed to be alert to people, and he communicated something very special. He was cared for at Great Ormond Street Children's Hospital and Birmingham Children's Hospital, and the nurses and other hospital staff loved him dearly. He came to church each Sunday with his family, and was a familiar little person in his pram. Lionel and Mary spoke in church about Jonathan and what he had given to them and taught them about life.

One evening I was called to the Birmingham Children's Hospital where Jonathan had been treated for an infection but was very sick. My colleague Tamsin and I arrived at the hospital to find the family gathered there, knowing that Jonathan was having difficulty breathing and had not been responding to powerful antibiotics. Not long afterwards, he caught a secondary infection which the antibiotics also failed to hit.

When Lionel and Mary were due to meet the consultants to discuss possible treatments, they asked me to go with them for support. The ITU consultant said that he and his team did not propose to undertake any invasive treatment, as they felt Jonathan would not benefit from it and it could add to his suffering. This was a great shock to Lionel and Mary, and they asked the consultants to allow them some time alone to think things through.

I realized that Mary had not had time to acknowledge or accept that Jonathan was dying; she needed time to come to terms with this and talk it out. She was not only a mother, but also the voice of her child who had no voice of his own. Her fear was that the medical staff were not able to accept that Jonathan had a quality of life and brought richness into many other people's lives. If he were not so severely disabled, she wondered, would a different decision be made about treatment? It was vital to face these issues with the doctors. It also seemed appropriate to call for a second opinion.

Further discussions with the consultants took place. The parents were able to voice their concerns, and they were listened to carefully. The consultants still felt that the ventilation treatment was unlikely to be successful and might cause harm and distress to Jonathan. After a long time of listening and discussion, the decision against treatment was made, and steps were taken to transfer Jonathan to the Acorns Children's Hospice, where the family were well known.

Jonathan died early the next morning with his family close by. The intervening hours had been very intense, but he died a beautiful death, surrounded by the love of his family, friends and nursing staff, and in his mother's bed. One of his special nurses had felt God say that he would have a beautiful death.

The next days were spent preparing for the funeral. It was a wonderful funeral, with some 300 or more people

– medics, nurses, family and friends – celebrating a special person with love, warmth and emotion. Lionel gave a very special word, the children led the prayers, and a young friend sang a beautiful song. There was much gratitude, joy and wonder at the way this little boy had changed our way of seeing.

A particular quote from Jürgen Moltmann expressed Mary's deep concern about how we view disability. Jonathan was severely disabled, yet behind what you saw was a lovely little person who could be loved and who gave love to others. Moltmann attacks the modern distinction that tends to distance healthy people from the disabled or handicapped. In reality there is no such thing as a non-handicapped life, but the ideal of health set up by a society of the capable condemns a certain group of people to be called handicapped:

> Our society arbitrarily defines health as the capacity for work and the capacity for enjoyment, but true health is something quite different. True health is the strength to live, the strength to suffer, and the strength to die. Health is not a condition of my body; it is the power of my soul to cope with the varying condition of that body.[9]

In that respect, every human life is limited, vulnerable and weak. It is this perspective of life that Jonathan's parents had wanted to share with the consultants, to ensure that their judgements and decisions always held that truth in mind. Jonathan's life was a kingdom state-ment that God's love and glory can bring strength out of

9 Jürgen Moltmann, *The Power of the Powerless* (SCM Press, 1983), p. 142.

weakness and beauty out of disability. Our perception is so often stunted because we consider that what *we* experience is normal – but other people's experience of life can be a gift to us that extends our horizons.

One consultant friend of Lionel and Mary wrote a tribute that was read out by his wife at the funeral service. This is what he wrote:

> I want to start by telling you how very sorry I am that I cannot come to Jonathan's thanksgiving service today. Jonathan was a unique individual, vulnerable and defenceless, who needed to be nurtured, cared for and protected. Yet I have always felt that he deserved so much more than pity – indeed Jonathan was a boy who was uniquely worthy, not just of compassion, but also of respect.
>
> . . . I knew Jonathan both as a friend and as a professional. He made such a strong impression on those who cared for him. How many times have I heard people at the hospital say 'Jonathan Mills and his family are amazing, aren't they?' So many of my colleagues have been touched by the fortitude with which he bore repeated and often painful medical intervention. He could cry – I know because I saw him do it – but how little he complained, no matter what he had to put up with.
>
> In many ways, I think he fulfilled an extraordinary ministry: Jonathan helped many people to examine themselves and to grow, whether they were Christians or not. Your son exercised a strong hold that will stay with many of us indelibly forever. You have much to be proud of in him.

When I visited the family, the children wanted to ask questions about death and what happens afterwards. It was also important to follow through some of the concerns that Lionel and Mary had following Jonathan's death. They were able to write a letter to the hospital, who offered to talk with them following Jonathan's death. That letter expressed their concern about how hospitals view disability, and raised particular questions which were still on their minds. Such follow-up is beneficial in terms of helping the bereaved to work through their grief, but it is also a path to improving the quality of communication and care in similar circumstances.

I am convinced that hospital chaplains – sometimes more so than parish priests – are in a position where they can begin to influence society's attitude to death and bring about a more healthy understanding, simply because they are where people die. They are also part of a team, and can therefore encourage all the members of that team to share their different perspectives and thus enrich each other's perceptions.

Jonathan's death had something powerful to say to our secular society about suffering and the gospel perspective on that subject. Christ's incarnation, life, death, resurrection, ascension and Second Coming give a perspective that is important to all of us today. It affirms that God is to be found in the midst of our journey, and we will touch all these moments at different points of our lives. It is this God who says, 'In all their distress he too was distressed, and the angel of his presence saved them' (Isaiah 63:9).

Other agencies

I have found it helpful to know something about the other caring agencies that can provide support to our parishioners in need. In their own fields of expertise, they offer a level of care that local churches may not be equipped to give, and some have made a very significant contribution to the support of the bereaved.

The work of the Society of Compassionate Friends, founded by the Revd Simon Stephens following his work with a family who lost their young son, helps families bereaved of children. His book *Death Comes Home*[10] has much common sense and practical help to offer to any who stand with those who weep for lost children.

Another society, Cruse, is the national organization supporting the widowed and their children. Founded by doctor's wife Margaret Torrie, the society has a national network of branches and invites widows and widowers to join. It provides a place where they can meet to share their feelings and problems and find support, and has made a real contribution to the care of the bereaved. Cruse also runs very good national and local training courses with leading authorities on dying and bereavement, and provides a helpful book list for further reference.

The Foundation for the Study of Infant Deaths exists to promote and sponsor research into 'cot deaths', and to support and counsel bereaved parents. At the time of writing, they provide two valuable leaflets – 'Information for the Parents of a Child who has Died Suddenly and Unexpectedly in Infancy', and 'Your Next Child'.[11] It would be valuable for clergy to have a supply of these, as they are specifically designed to help grieving parents. If feelings of fear, guilt and blame are not faced, the pressure on the marriage can be such that it

10 Simon Stephens, *Death Comes Home* (Mowbrays, 1972).
11 FSID, 11–19 Artillery Row, London SW1P 1RT,
   www.fsid@sids.org.uk

will lead to its breakdown. So many counselling needs go back to unresolved grief in early life.

The Hospice Movement, made famous by the work of Dr Cicely Saunders and Dr Richard Lamerton, has made a huge contribution to the care of the dying and the bereaved. Saunders' and Lamerton's concern was to provide support in this experience of life and to ensure that it is a family affair. Both the dying and the bereaved are helped through that process. There is also a home-care scheme, which covers patients in the area and provides back-up beds. This enables many to be cared for and to die in their own homes, knowing there is round-the-clock care on call. The Hospice Movement has helped to educate and inform both doctors and the public in better care, yet it needs more support and government finance so that it can continue to develop. Dr Cicely Saunders' book *The Management of Terminal Illness* and Dr Lamerton's *Care of the Dying* are important works in this field.[12]

Lastly the Samaritans, which grew out of Dr Chad Vara's counselling ministry, are well known for their care and support of any who are experiencing a particular crisis in their lives.

Each of these societies or movements has sprung from personal initiative in response to the particular needs of the dying and the bereaved. They have all provided a greater insight, understanding and care for those experiencing this particular transition, and pastors would do well to learn from them and use their services whenever appropriate.

---

12 Dame Cicely Saunders, *Management of Terminal Illness* (E. Arnold, 1978). R. Lamerton, *Care of the Dying* (Priory Press, 1980).

6

Towards a Theology of Hope

The questions 'What have I done to deserve this?' or 'Why has God allowed this to happen to me?' represent both an attempt to make sense of the experience of bereavement and a sense of hopelessness. Faced with bereavement, we ask such questions as an expression of our yearning for truth and meaning.

In seeking to stand with the bereaved in their loss, we do well to remember C. S. Lewis's description of God as 'the great Iconoclast'.[1] He cannot be confined to an idea, for when we try to do that he shatters the idea or image by which we represent him. The example of Job's suffering or Jesus' incarnation show the iconoclastic God shattering inadequate answers to questions raised by man in his deepest need. As we try to discover hope in the experience of loss, we therefore need to be careful of futile or trite statements, which can only hurt the sufferer and discredit the God we represent. We need to beware of an unhealthy religion that can be offered lightly to heal the wounds of the bereaved but fails to

---

1 Lewis, *A Grief Observed*, p. 52.

point the sufferer forward to a new life. We must not be guilty of being the kind of false prophet or priest described by Jeremiah:

> They dress the wound of my people
> as though it were not serious.
> 'Peace, peace,' they say,
> when there is no peace. (Jeremiah 8:11)

Bereavement as opportunity

Experiences of loss can be opportunities either for growth and maturity or for stagnation and disintegration. Edgar Jackson speaks of this dual possibility in an illustration from nature:

> On our farm, we have a row of maple trees that illustrate the mysterious processes of adaptation. Many years ago the trees were used as fence posts for the stringing of barbed wire around the pasture. Now, fifty or sixty years later it is possible to look at those trees and observe the way the life process shows itself in adaptation. In some places, the trees fought against the barbed wire as a hostile agent, and here the trees have long and ugly scars that deface the bark and inner structure of the trees. In other places, there is quite a different form of adaptation. The barbed wire has been accepted and incorporated into the life of the tree. Where this has happened the barbed wire left no mark on the tree, and after all these years all that shows is the wire entering on one side and exiting at the other. It looks as if there has been a small hole bored through the tree and the wire carefully inserted.[2]

---

2 Jackson, *The Many Faces of Grief*, p. 123.

The illustration begs the question, why is it that some of the trees injured themselves, whereas others incorporated the injuring object and made it an experience for growth? Bereavement is a loss. It is a minus not a plus, a great aching void, a hole, a vacuum. How can one build on a hole? Is there a way in which the hole can be filled so that building can begin again? Is there hope, or only despair? If the deprivation is to be turned to advantage or growth, the tragedy turned to triumph, then it seems that two things are vital:

1. The hole must be acknowledged – reality must be faced.
2. The hole must be filled – it must be recognized that there is hope of moving forward.

If such a positive goal is to be realized, it will depend on the resources available within the bereaved and their ability to accept support as they try to face their loss. That movement forward is not a recovery of what has been lost, but a relinquishing of it, so that a fresh experience can be entered, in which the past has been integrated and becomes a means of influencing and enriching the present.

Before we look at these two factors, it is worth mentioning that it is extremely important to take every advantage of change in life's experience, so that we may be better prepared to face greater areas of change when they occur. It is therefore important for parents to equip their children to expect and to manage change in their growth process, for change is an inevitable part of life. From the experience of birth, through weaning and onwards, children experience loss and change. When they are prepared for this and helped through it, they will be better equipped to cope with more painful change in the future.

Acknowledging the hole

First, then, it is important to face reality – the hole must be acknowledged. William Blake wrote,

> Man was made for Joy and Woe,
> And when this we rightly know,
> Thro' the world we safely go.
> Joy and Woe were woven fine,
> A clothing for the soul divine.[3]

The poem speaks of the integration of each experience into the whole of life, forming a tapestry in which the weaver makes a design from all the threads. Much human frustration and sickness is the result of attempts to evade pain, which instead needs to be faced and endured. In the experience of grief it is natural at first to deny the loss and to feel that it is an illusion – but what seems like an illusion is real, and the ritual of the funeral helps to make that apparent. Pastors can best help by assisting the bereaved to acknowledge the facts as they are, not as they would wish them to be, and to begin to react to that reality. The truth opens the way to progress. Mourning can only begin when the loss has been realized.

Facing the reality of loss is hard, however, because of the pain and fear of what it might lead to. In his Gospel,

---

3 William Blake, *Auguries of Innocence* (*c.* 1803), ll. 56–60.

John expresses our natural inclination to avoid the way of suffering: 'But when you are old you will stretch out your hands, and someone else will dress you and lead you where you do not want to go' (John 21:18).

We live in a society that seeks to avoid or ignore suffering, difficulty or hardship of any kind, but with that we also avoid the opportunities to develop maturity, endurance and character. We can try to dismiss the onset of loss as little more than an unpleasant interlude, thinking that at best it will simply go away of its own accord, or at worst it can somehow be contained. We can deny what is happening to us by taking refuge in compulsive activity, or by resorting to some coping technique that satisfactorily handled a crisis in the past.

Gerald O'Collins describes a man who struggled in just this way to fend off the reality of loss: 'I worked harder and drank too much. I kept resisting but finally the pain overwhelmed me. And I let it happen.' He fled the issues, but ultimately he had to take them in hand and deal with them.

If we are to move through grief, we must take the risk of letting go. It is only as we do this and open ourselves to the experience of loss that we can be broken, remade and restructured to live in the present moment. We cannot mend our world when it comes apart at the seams. We should rather let it come apart – even at the cost of pain – and it is when we do so that we accept death and experience resurrection.

Mary Craig, in her book *Blessings*, illustrates the truth of entering into pain and discovering hope and meaning. Mary had four sons, two of whom were particularly deprived. Paul suffered from Hohler's syndrome (or gargoylism) and Nicky had Down's syndrome. Her book describes her pilgrimage through pain and her search for meaning. She speaks of the massive pain of that second blow when Nicky was born:

> When Frank came to see me that afternoon, he could not trust himself to speak, any more than I could. He held my hand, while we both stayed silent, frightened by the enormity of the blow and the collapse of our hopes. Even now, years later, we have never told each other what we felt when we first heard the news. They are feelings too deep for sharing.[4]

She describes herself as slipping into the abyss, spinning in an endlessly twisting spiral. It was when she had given up hope of ever reaching the bottom that some words she had read flashed into her mind: 'Our tragedy is not that we suffer, but that we waste suffering. We waste the opportunity of growing into compassion.' These words halted the seeming slide into madness and gave her a sense of being held firm, safe from further falling. A voice inside was saying, 'There is a way through this, but you must find it outside of yourself. Remember I am here, in the darkness. You are never alone.'[5] It was there in the abyss, in the hole, that she discovered she was not alone – God was present.

Filling the hole

The second factor vital to recovery is that there must be hope that the vacuum can be filled. As we enter into the

4 Mary Craig, *Blessings* (Hodder & Stoughton, 1979), p. 60.
5 *Ibid.*, p. 61.

abyss, we need to know that there is the possibility of discovering comfort, strength and healing. This hope may come through a sense of meeting God, or it may come through seeing hope in others and being strengthened by their example.

To me, this is the meaning of the Christian hope founded on the life, death and resurrection of Jesus Christ. He gives significance to life. He lived in the awareness of his life being held in God's control, knowing that nothing could happen unless permitted by his Father. Jesus spoke of the fruit that is born of suffering: 'Unless a grain of wheat falls to the ground and dies, it remains only a single seed. But if it dies, it produces many seeds' (John 12:24). He also affirmed the experience of loss and mourning, standing with Martha and Mary in their grief. First Martha and then Mary said to him, 'If you had been here, my brother would not have died,' and Jesus wept with them (John 11:21, 32, 35).

Jesus, however, chose not to stop death, but to conquer it by entering into that experience and facing that vacuum. Thus in his life and death we realize the cosmic presence of God. He is not only out there, he is here with us. As we enter fully into life, and its suffering and loss, we may encounter him – the wounded healer, the crucified God. He shares with us in our suffering and also shares with us the fruits of his victory. The hole is filled as we meet the one who entered the vacuum of hope – 'in order to fill the whole universe' (Ephesians 4:10). We discover the comfort of God through the wounded healer; we meet resurrection in the reality of death, and we are promised the continuing presence of God in a new awareness of the Spirit.

It seems to me that there is a great pastoral opportunity

in all this for helping the bereaved. I have found on numerous occasions that people can speak of some kind of mystical experience, a dream or vision, which they have been unable to interpret but from which they have drawn great strength. We should *expect* God to be at work in these crisis events; we should be looking for the signs of his coming and ready to interpret their meaning to the bereaved. Our concern should be that this becomes a continuing experience of God, rather than a recollection that remains just a memory but leads to nothing more.

Carlo Carretto describes the experience of trial and transition beautifully:

> This soldering, made with the fire of sorrow on the cleft of man's poverty . . . becomes the meeting place, the bridge of passage, the terrain of the invisible kingdom of God. God meets man at the crossroads of his poverty, in the bowl of his hunger, in the thirst of his need, in the realisation of his limits as a creature, in the agony of his death. And he meets him to give him what he is searching for.[6]

It is when God meets us in this experience that building for the future can truly begin. The experience of resurrection is not only a future promise, but also a present reality. It is the call to follow the one who has lived life and given it its true meaning. It is not the struggle to make life an event of meaning – it is the inner rest to receive the gift of life and let God show us the way forward. From this foundation of peace a new life can be built in the fellowship of God's people.

---

6   Carlo Carretto, *The God Who Comes* (Orbis Books, 1995) p. 228.

From my reflections on 34 years of ministry, I know that there is an immense pastoral opportunity afforded by crisis events to help people discover the meaning and purpose of life. The church has a huge responsibility to help society towards a healthier attitude to death. Those in pastoral ministry need to promote a better understanding in families and schools of children's particular need when faced with bereavement. We also have a great opportunity to use the rites of passage to assist people in working through the grief process.

Sadly, society often tries to rush that process, because it cannot bear the pain involved of journeying with others through grief and pain. Yet we must avoid the temptation to hinder the journey towards wholeness in which the bereaved can pick up the shattered pieces and integrate them into the present. The psalmist speaks beautifully of that process:

> Blessed are those whose strength is in you,
> who have set their hearts on pilgrimage.
> As they pass through the Valley of Baca,
> they make it a place of springs;
> the autumn rains also cover it with pools.
> They go from strength to strength. (Psalm 84:5–7)

7

Changing Churches

The process of a pastor leaving a church and moving to a new church is often a vulnerable transition which needs careful management. Either no one can match the previous pastor, with the result that the church is often looking backwards and fails to move on, or the new man is a figure facing huge expectations. Often congregations will be hoping that the new person will wave a wand and all will be rosy. The truth, however, is that the reality of the situations at both old and new churches has to be faced and worked through before things can move forward.

The importance of listening

Great wisdom was shown by the prophet Ezekiel when the Lord sent him to be a messenger among the exiles, having told him to speak only his word. 'I came to the exiles who lived at Tel Abib near the Kebar River. And there, where they were living, I sat among them for seven days – overwhelmed' (Ezekiel 3:15). During those seven days Ezekiel listened, sensing where those people were and discerning in his spirit what God was saying. From that listening, he became aware of the word of the Lord coming to him, perhaps as he was asking questions of God.

I believe pastors can learn something important from this picture. There is great wisdom in listening to where the church is and hearing what people are saying, both positive and negative. Such listening should include a wide spectrum of church members, and it is vital to ask God for his discernment at the same time. Sometimes those who wish to bend the ear of a new incumbent may not be those who see things from the clearest perspective.

There will be different forces at work in a church, some wanting to turn things back, others to move forward too hastily. In such a situation, taking stock before turning to action has to be the wisest course. Having said that, occasionally there may be some urgent and long overdue action that is required, and such decisions should not be postponed.

When I came to St John's, Harborne, I was acutely aware of the expectations of change. I come from a naval family, and one image that immediately came to mind was that of a large ship changing course: a huge vessel such as a tanker or aircraft carrier will be several miles down the sea lane before that course alteration takes full effect. I also remembered going to sea as a 15-year-old on a naval cruiser which had undergone a refit. It was time for the sea trials, in which the crew were involved in intensive exercises, learning to act as a unit and to deploy all the new equipment and weaponry. The purpose was to turn them into an effective team, a fighting force ready for action.

recorded tapes. A visit from the Fisherfolk[2] in 1975 was a very significant moment for St John's, because it underlined the values of worship that were already being laid down, and also provided a considerable impetus from outside. It lifted the experience of worship to a new plane, and for a number of years worship became a central focus of the church, as a sacrifice of praise to God.

The growth of the church was accompanied by an increase in the staff team to three clergy, which with three lay people formed an eldership, meeting together weekly. Nonetheless, the demands of the growing church were huge, bringing a heavy pastoral load and requiring wise leadership. The weight on the staff, and especially on Tom Walker, was considerable.

Tom encouraged and allowed people to take risks, with his support. He particularly encouraged young people in leadership and engagement with issues of social justice. Their walks for Shelter and work with street children brought many problems, however, and this added extra pressure while both the leadership and the young people learned how to handle stress from people of different cultural outlooks, as well as from church members who found the activities disturbing.

Much criticism was directed at the vicar during this time. Despite this, many who were out of their depth were driven to prayer, and they saw God doing some

2 Fisherfolk were the worship group from the Church of the Redeemer, Houston, Texas, developed under the rector Graham Pulkingham. They had experienced a renewal of church life in a downtown area of Houston, and formed homes as a basis of community life.

wonderful things in changed lives. Some significant healings took place, and a number of demonized people were delivered and set free. Tom was significantly used in this ministry. God was manifestly at work, but spiritual warfare was a reality. Moreover, the movement into renewal exposed division. Some went with it; others drew back in criticism and fear; some left the church altogether.

A very significant decision was taken when St John's took on St Germaine's, a local church with a redundancy order on it. About 40 young people joined that church from St John's, some moving house into the parish and effectively establishing a church plant. Tom appointed a member of staff to lead it, and continued to offer wise support. By the time he left, the curate appointed to St Germaine's had become priest-in-charge, and later became its vicar, with the church becoming an independent parish. This was an important step, and the process was taken as a model of church planting in the diocese, opening the way forward for other schemes to take place.

By the mid 1980s, however, the renewal had lost its impetus. The spontaneity and vigour had gone, though the impact and ministry of the church was still considerable. Those who had been added to the church would not have noticed the difference, but those who had been there since the early 1970s were aware that the momentum was running out. Tom suffered from ill health and stress for the last five years of his time at St John's, and was also burdened with extra responsibility in the diocese as a rural dean and as chair of the House of Clergy. To some extent, those last years were hard for vicar and people, in that the degree of hurt and disappointment in the church could not be acknowledged openly and thus find some degree of resolution.

A chapter in Tom's book *Small Streams, Big Rivers* highlights some of the problems the church encountered. It reflects a true picture of the hurt among the leaders, which Tom discussed with the bishop.

> Things could not have been worse at this time. We seemed to be divided up into factions. As a leader I was heavily under criticism. Where there should have been a loving fellowship and unity, there was appalling criticism and backbiting. In reacting to the complaints with hard words I was not exempt from blame.
>
> 'Can you conceive it possible that a group of Christian people can destroy each other with bitter and jealous words? I'm at my wits' end and do not know where to turn to next. Do I cave in and leave the parish or fight it through?'
>
> 'You neither run away nor fight,' the Bishop wisely advised. 'You simply accept the situation. You accept that this is what the ministry is all about.'[3]

People's loyalty to the church meant that not many left, but instead continued to support and give to a church experiencing disappointment and pain.

Contributing factors

It is important to explore some of the factors that might have contributed to that disappointment and loss of momentum, because such reflection gives energy to deal

3 Tom Walker, *Small Streams, Big Rivers* (Scripture Union, 1991), pp. 137–8.

with mistakes and make them creative for the future.

One significant factor was that the increased size of the congregation meant that two morning services had to be held, and this subdued the overall intimacy and unity of the church. Moreover, the structures for growth, particularly the small group arrangements, were perhaps not fully in place to nurture and sustain that growth.

Another telling factor was that a very strong style of leadership did not sit easily alongside a delegated structure such as an eldership. The eldership – three clergy and three laypeople – had been carefully and prayerfully considered and chosen in 1975, but it ran into difficulties because the expectations on both sides were so different. On an away day, the elders and their wives met with the clergy to share honestly where they thought the church was. This involved some constructive criticism which was very painful for the vicar and his wife.

The eldership continued, with the vicar appointing others, but something had gone out of the heart of it and the key figures were left damaged. Lack of open relationships in the leadership continued to dog the church. A fear of 'rocking the boat' meant that much emotion was suppressed, incurring a destructive long-term effect. The failure to speak the truth in love and to face conflict as a creative part of being community deprived the church of the capacity to resolve these painful issues.

The problem was that the pressure on a large church to succeed meant that failures were not easily admitted. The church was a professional congregation with high standards. Fear of failure prevented a number of people from offering their gifts and learning from their mistakes. When I arrived at St John's there were no clergy colleagues, though Geoff Lanham joined me five months later. I remember that we made a mistake with the appointment of a children's leader. It was obvious in hindsight that this was the case, and we decided to own up to the mistake and rectify it publicly. A warden commented afterwards that he had never heard such a public admission before, but he felt that, if the leadership could acknowledge mistakes, then it was safe to trust them. Winston Churchill's definition of success has much significance for me: 'Success is the ability to move from failure to failure without loss of enthusiasm.'

In the latter years of Tom's time there, the staff relationships between the curates were difficult and known to be so. This undoubtedly affected the unity of the church, as people took sides and a partisan spirit developed. As a result, the leadership became less open and vulnerable and at times reacted in hurt, thereby compounding that hurt. This was apparent sometimes from the pulpit, with particular stances and attitudes being attacked.

When we moved to the church and settled into our new home, we noticed immediately that people did not visit the vicarage. They seemed to be nervous and fearful of coming inside. This seemed strange to us, but highlighted the degree of disturbance that had taken place in the psyche of the church.

In later times, some of the activities initiated did not necessarily come out of a previous listening to God. The church was well resourced financially and in terms of personnel, and therefore could make things happen. One instance of this was a Saltmine Mission in which people expended huge energy on inviting friends to supper parties and concerts. This proved to be singularly unfruitful, and many Christian folk felt let down because they felt they had burned their boats with their friends. A further complicating factor was that the issue of evaluating the mission was not addressed. Many swallowed their negative feelings towards evangelism, only for them to resurface some years later, when we were exploring Alpha as a model of evangelism. The explosive reaction to this on the part of some made us deeply aware of unresolved issues needing to be addressed. One elder expressed a hint of this, commenting on the disappointment of that earlier mission. Another said, 'I'm so glad you said that. I thought I was the only one who felt that.'

One curate perceptively commented that when he arrived in 1987 he felt the church was at the 'back end of renewal'. He perceived that while the church preached 'grace', it lived under 'Law'. He sensed a hardening of the 'oughteries', which made the fellowship a harsh and judging community. The church was frenetically busy in running so many things, but this covered up a lack of the breath of the Spirit. It was reminiscent of the Galatian experience of following the Spirit and then coming under the yoke of the Law (Galatians 3:1–35).

The church and its leaders had been wounded, and because this had not been faced, there was no way of resolving it – and help from outside was not considered. The church that had been a pioneer of renewal had lost something of the joy and freedom of the Spirit. There was a lack of stimulus from other church leaders in renewal, and hence a lack of the invigoration that cross-fertilization gives. Without realizing it, the church had moved into a backwater.

Another indication of the ebbing of the renewal was that the spontaneity and creativity that marked the early renewal had gone. This was manifest in the loss of freedom in worship and the earlier creativity that was apparent in music, dance and spontaneous testimonies of what God was doing. In the area of the charismatic gifts of the Spirit, people did not feel safe to step out and take risks.

When we reflected on all this, we realized that the ebbing of renewal was like the tide going out. It left some debris on the beach that needed to be cleared up, so that the church would be ready to catch the tide when it next came in. That process seems to be part of the economy of God.

Moving into a new phase

The interregnum following Tom Walker's departure gave the church an opportunity to take stock and prepare for a new phase. It proved to be a positive time, in which the elders and the curates were able to own and address some of the problems in the leadership and the church which had not been faced and resolved earlier.

The church was called to pray over the new appointment, for there was a fear that the patrons (the Church Society) would seek to appoint someone from the conservative evangelical tradition, taking the church back to its past and undoing the very significant years of renewal. Such an appointment would not fit with the church's position. The following year was largely taken up with the process of the appointment, with many

names being referred and no appointment being made.
The church drew together to pray earnestly about
the matter.

The elders met one day to pray in the church, and
sensed the need to pray over the wounds and disappointments the church had been through. They prayed
through the whole church building with confession and
repentance. During this period a Ugandan clergyman
(Revd John Magumba) came to Birmingham for a year's
study and joined the staff team. He was spiritually very
discerning, and he sensed spiritual oppression and the
need for prayer to break certain strongholds. Coming
from outside, he spoke right into the situation in a way
that the elders discerned was right.

In the past leaders had been oppressed and some
moral sin had occurred. A number of curates or their
wives had suffered either emotional or physical stress
during their time in the church. The present curates had
experienced a difficult relationship with each other due
to a lack of clarity in their roles, insecurity and a com-
petitive spirit. This division also affected the
congregation.

During the interregnum, however, a visiting speaker
led a church weekend in which the Holy Spirit powerfully touched the staff team, resulting in reconciliation.
This was a very positive experience for the congregation
and a sign of hope. Both curates found new appoint-
ments before the interregnum was concluded, leaving a
non-stipendiary minister and the elders holding the fort.
This meant that a fresh start could be made with the
new incumbent.

Some six months later, we were called to consider the
living and were offered the job. I remember being asked

by the elders whether I sensed God was saying anything to us about the church. I had an impression of the story of Aslan, from C. S. Lewis's *The Lion, the Witch and the Wardrobe*, where the characters had been turned to stone. Aslan breathed on them and they came alive. I sensed that St John's had lost its breath and needed a fresh breath from God. The elders were sure this was right, and it confirmed to them that it was right to invite us to come. We also sensed such openness and hunger, and knew that this was the place to which God was leading us.

At our last service at St Andrew's, High Wycombe, the congregation took time to gather round to pray and listen to God. One lady called Lyn had a picture of an ambulance rushing up the M40 with a heart transplant. That image is one that has never left me, and it seemed so apt. At St John's we met many people, including leaders, who felt isolated and lonely. There seemed to be a lack of family warmth, a lack of the kind of atmosphere in which people could safely fail, grow and take risks. We hoped, with God, to set about bringing a new heart to that church.

8

Addressing the Present and the Past

In this chapter we shall look at how we face and address wounds of the past so that they do not hold us back from moving forward. The letters to the seven churches in Revelation give examples of how the word of prophecy can warn a church that is in danger, and needs to address issues that could extinguish its light and witness to the world.

Our experience of coming to St John's was twofold: first, it was one of loss, as we left behind a lively, risk-taking community with whom we had shared a 15-year journey of faith; second, it was one of excitement, as we wondered what could happen next. St John's Church is a wonderful community situated near the University and the Queen Elizabeth Hospital, with numbers of international students from all over the world.

Unresolved issues

At my induction in 1992 Bishop Mark Santer preached prophetically over the church. The day was the 17th January, the festival of St Anthony of Egypt. As it happens, I was born in Alexandria, Egypt. Bishop Mark spoke of the hermit's life of prayer and the influence he wrought. Once when Anthony was asked about the secret to his life, he lifted up his outstretched hand to heaven, saying, 'Would that we were all fire.' Bishop Mark lifted up his own hands heavenward, saying, 'Would that St John's were all fire.' I felt a quickening in my spirit that this was what God wanted to do in St John's – little did I realize the purging and pain that would be part of that purifying process. The bishop also said to me in private conversation that he would love St John's to be known in the High Street and bear an influence in the community. The truth was that the church had not impacted its immediate community, though it was well known and had borne an influence in the church far and wide.

Very early in my time here, it became obvious to me that there were a number of unresolved issues requiring attention. The first year or more involved much prayer with church members, dealing with hurts and disappointments, and on a number of occasions hearing confessions of moral failure which had remained concealed but must have weakened the Christian community.

As a result of these unresolved issues, some of which spread over a number of years, there was a feeling of isolation, a word I heard repeatedly mentioned. People spoke of not feeling they belonged, of not being accepted, and many spoke of not 'feeling safe' in the church family.

This surprised me, as individually members were gifted, competent and warm-hearted, but the general atmosphere was inclined to be judgemental. Isolation, disappointment and despair were words frequently used by members of the church to describe how they felt.

Some time after our arrival in Birmingham, my wife experienced a depth of intercession that she had not known before. Often in the church or at home she would find herself weeping when she prayed, without knowing why. A key to understanding what was happening was given by Phyllida Mould, a friend who had founded the Ffald-y-Brenin retreat centre in Wales and had a significant prayer and prophetic ministry. She phoned out of the blue one morning to say that she had been praying for us and had a dream in which both of us were climbing a steep hill shrouded in dark mist.

In the dream I was wearing a wet suit, and she believed God was saying this so I could climb ahead and get on with the job he had given me to do. Anne, however, in the dream was shrouded in dark mist and Phyllida sensed God say this was so Anne could feel the darkness and despair of the people and cry out for them. Phyllida had had no idea that Anne had already been doing this. This was a great encouragement and gave us a better understanding of prophetic prayer, or the groaning Paul describes as the prayer 'that words cannot express' in Romans 8:26. Some time later, other people in the church experienced the same kind of intercessory prayer coming upon them.

We became aware that there had been a cycle of verbal violence in the church over a period of time.[1] Things had been said from the pulpit in anger and staff had been equally hurt by criticism. The result was a

---

1 See Walker, *Small Streams, Big Rivers*, p. 135.

withdrawal from one another and a development of defensive postures. Such negative words leave a mark, and lead to mistrust, which I knew needed healing – but we could not at first see how to do so without seeming to judge what had happened or to be disloyal to the church's past.

The importance of thanksgiving

As I pondered on how to break this cycle of verbal abuse, I was struck by something I read in Dietrich Bonhoeffer's book on community, *Life Together*. Speaking about the practice of daily thanksgiving in the community of faith, he says that if we criticize, we hinder God from letting our church grow according to the measure and riches that are there for all of us in Christ Jesus. He then goes on to say,

> This applies in a special way to the complaints often heard from pastors and zealous members about their congregations. A pastor should not complain about his congregation, certainly never to other people, but also not to God. A congregation has not been entrusted to him in order that he should become its accuser before God and men.[2]

If we start to speak against each other, or against those for whom we have responsibility, we cut ourselves off from being a helpmeet to those people. We push them further into darkness, where not only the accuser of the brethren is able to abuse them, but we also stand against

---

2 Dietrich Bonhoeffer, *Life Together* (SCM, 1949), p. 17.

them. God has given us the privilege of standing in the gap so that we might help them with our prayers, not our judgement. The best way we can help individuals to grow is to bring them with thanksgiving into the presence of God; to pray for them, recognizing that they are in a covenant relationship with God and therefore in the way of salvation. This allows the grace of God to come to them bringing the possibility of change.

I would like to share three examples, from different periods of my ministry, in which I learned more about how to facilitate owning and dealing with past hurt and anger in the church, drawing out the poison and alienation in order to let it go and to allow a healing to take place.

Using symbolism to release past hurt

On the first occasion, I learned the value and importance of symbolism in ministering to people's hidden needs. Our church, coming from a strong Protestant tradition, had no symbols of the faith – no cross, candles or anything like that. On Good Friday, however, I decided to use a large cross that fitted into a stand. Using verses from Isaiah 53 – 'Surely he took up our infirmities and carried our sorrows . . . he was pierced for our transgressions, he was crushed for our iniquities' (vv. 4–5) – I spoke of Jesus carrying our sins as well as our sorrows. This included the things we had done, and the things others had done to us. In a time for reflection, I encouraged people to write down the things they wanted to nail to the cross, and then bring their pieces of paper to the cross and hammer them in, symbolizing a 'letting go'. It was very moving to see a hundred or more people queuing to hammer their burdens to the cross. On the centrepiece one member had written, 'I hate the church.' That letting go is a process, however, and the layers of debris needed further time and opportunity for response.

The second occasion when conflict between leaders and people was released concerned the symbol of the shepherd's staff. As a minister I was aware how, as shepherds with our own insecurities, we can hurt our people, and I sensed a need to address this. My colleague Geoff Lanham was to preach on Ezekiel 34, and as a way of responding to the word, we decided to ask the people's forgiveness for those occasions when we or our predecessors had abused our leadership authority.

To symbolize this I went into the congregation with a shepherd's staff, asking forgiveness for times when we and other leaders might have abused our spiritual authority. We then held several shepherd's staffs at the sanctuary steps, while people could come up and kneel, holding the staff and then choosing to let it go when they were ready, symbolizing forgiveness and letting go of a past conflict. These symbolic actions allowed people to express before God the weight of the suppressed feelings they had been carrying, which hindered both them and the church. This was an important moment in our church's life. Many people came forward for prayer – some in considerable distress from past experiences – and received healing at different levels.

Understanding a church's roots

The third occasion came in the summer of 1995, when I was preaching a series on the letters to the seven churches in Revelation. These studies were immensely significant for releasing the church. The seven letters highlight the church's need for the prophetic word, as a means of encouraging what is good and pinpointing issues that need to be addressed. While reading Walter Wink's trilogy, *Naming the Powers*, *Unmasking the Powers* and *Engaging the Powers*,[3] I was struck by the way he addresses issues of domination and attitudes that can infect a church or organization.

I have learnt that every church has its story of birth and development. This story has a real effect on the continuing life of the church, influencing its identity and shaping its future development. Within each story are particular strengths and weaknesses that affect the group story of the church. If you do not discern these rightly, you will be struggling against roots that will undermine what you are trying to address on the surface.

Wink describes various examples of churches that seem to be riven by strife and in continual conflict. Such conflicts can go back generations. Some churches have gone through many ministers, but Wink notes that the primary reason for such strife is congregational conflict that existed before the current pastor arrived. 'What appeared to be a personnel issue was, in fact, often a case of a strife-torn angel. The pastor was made a scapegoat for deeper conflicts that no one was willing to face.'[4] Sometimes church leaders or bishops have not recognized that what they have seen on the surface has an underlying root, which will continue to hold the church captive to its past if it is not addressed.

---

3 Fortress Press, 1984, 1986 and 1992 respectively.
4 Wink, *Unmasking the Powers*, pp. 76–77.

Wink quotes an example of an English bishop who was trying to merge two rural churches on the east coast where, a thousand years earlier, the Danes had invaded the country. The bishop tried repeatedly to merge the two congregations and appoint a single rector, but the people consistently refused. Finally, he went to one of the churches and said, 'You have told me many reasons why you don't want to merge with the other congregation, but none of them seems very convincing. Now tell me – what is your real reason?' One older member of the congregation replied, 'Well, Bishop, if you really want to know, they didn't tell us the Danes were coming.' He was referring to one church that had a 100-foot tower and saw the invaders approaching, but did not warn the other village, which suffered greatly from a marauding attack. With a memory that long, there was little chance of a merger without an act of apology and a response of forgiveness that would allow the memory to be buried. I have discovered that many churches similarly have long memories!

The early theologians interpreted the angels of Revelation 1–3 as spiritual guardians of the churches.[5] To enable a church to be released, we must discover our church story and, where necessary, bring release and healing so that we may move forward to fulfil God's purpose for the church.

The example of the Revelation churches

The letters to the seven churches provide a wonderful model of this dynamic at work. Jesus is addressing the group story of each church and challenging it to change.

---

5 *Ibid.*, p. 70, concerning Gregory of Nazianzus.

He addresses the angel of the church, and highlights strengths as well as weaknesses or sins that need to be challenged because they contain the seeds that can destroy the church. He makes a promise about what the future can be if the church will both hear and act.

Wink discusses with great insight the phrase 'the angel of the church'.[6] The angel is addressed in the singular – 'To the angel of the church . . . write . . .' (see e.g. Revelation 2:1). Each angel has a church in its care. It is interesting to note that, although the angel is addressed, the message then carries straight on to the whole congregation. Wink interprets the angel not as a human being or bishop of the church:

> It would appear that the angel is something separate from the congregation but must somehow represent it as a totality. The fact that the angel is addressed suggests that it is more than a personification of the church, but the actual spirituality of the congregation as a single entity. The angel would then exist in, with, and under the material expressions of the church's life as its interiority. The angel would have no separate existence apart from the people and conversely the people would have no unity apart from the angel. Angel and people are the inner and outer aspect of one and the same reality.[7]

Wink sees the angel as the embodiment of the spiritual story of the church, representing the group story in a single entity. I have found from my own experience that this interpretation gives a genuine understanding of the corporate personality or character of a church, shaped

6 *Ibid.*, pp. 69–86.
7 *Ibid.*, p. 70.

and developed by its experiences, leaders and choices. In dealing with a church, we are not dealing with a sum of individuals but with a corporate body of people who influence and affect one another and are affected by the environment and community to which they belong.

What is going on in these seven churches is far from ideal. Strife, factionalism, backbiting and heresy are rife. As human communities, some have little to commend them. The angels encompass both the good and the bad. They hold together 'what the church is, and what it is called to be'. What Wink is speaking of here is the reality of 'where the church is' in the present moment, but also the vocation of the church, 'what it is called to become'. That vocation is encoded in its DNA. If we are to bring healing to the church and change its persona, we have to honestly face where the church is and what has contributed to that expression. Such a process will be costly and painful because it requires that we face our wounds. We will need to confess the truth and forgive or ask forgiveness, so that we can begin to take the necessary steps to help the church recover its God-given vocation. The future promise for each church becomes possible when they respond in repentance to the prophetic word given to them. When I read this it confirmed to me the important process in which we were involved, as we sought to release the church from infected attitudes that poisoned the circulation of the body of Christ and were dangerous to leave untreated.

Discerning the health of the church

Wink asserts that it is important to discern the angel of the church and to gauge whether it is healthy or sick. We can do that by seeing what is reflected in the 'outward manifestation' of the life of the congregation. This can be seen in what the church building itself expresses and how it is cared for. It can also be reflected in the people, their socio-economic class and the values they espouse. It can be helpful to think of key words that describe something of the feel of the church and its personality: what it is now and what it can become.

The pastor's leadership style can also have an effect on the angel. 'Pastors can have a significant impact on the angel; all too often, unfortunately, that impact is the result of a dominating personality or an authoritarian style and not of a genuine angelic transformation.'[8] The people, who will often seek to avoid conflict at all costs, can respond to the weaknesses or insecurity of their minister. In my own experience, I have known times when my insecurity has hindered the growth and development of the congregation. I see this as a constant issue in healthy church leadership.

One of the clearest indicators of the health of an angel is how the congregation handles conflict. If conflict is not faced or rightly owned and expressed, it will break out in destructive ways. This pattern can stretch back a very long time. It may be that for a season, a period of years when the life of the Spirit is strong, negative patterns can be held in abeyance or overcome, but if the spiritual life of the church deteriorates, those negative patterns will resurface.

I remember leading a church weekend in Essex under the title 'New Wine – New Wineskins'. The church had a new vicar and some years earlier had known significant

---

8 *Ibid.*, p. 75.

growth, with two churches planted in the parish. We picked up the fact that many looked back to those days, but also felt a degree of hurt from the way the plants had happened and the draught felt by the mother church, which lost most of its leaders to the newly planted churches. That distrust and ill feeling surfaced at the weekend and in the evening service the vicar apologized for any hurt that his own or any previous leadership had caused. This met with a very moving response and cleared away much of the hurt, providing a way forward and a foundation on which to build.

I mentioned earlier that a pastor may be made a scapegoat for deeper conflicts that no one is willing to face.[9] An Anglican minister I counselled was vicar in a parish in Wales. He was effectively driven out of the church, because two churches that had been joined together by the bishop refused to work together. They resisted all the vicar's attempts at mission or at reaching out to the community. He discovered to his horror that during the interregnum the PCC had voted against holding prayer meetings or any evangelism in the parish.

Later he stumbled across fraud by a churchwarden who also had an alcohol problem. Feeling that it was inappropriate for the warden to assist at Communion when he was often worse the wear for drink, the vicar mentioned the situation to the archdeacon, who promptly withdrew the warden's licence to assist at Communion. While he was on holiday, the PCC passed a vote of no confidence in the vicar, and after that sent weekly letters that wore him down. Eventually he

---

9 *Ibid.*, p. 77.

162 THE PASTOR'S NOTEBOOK

resigned, the fourth vicar to do so in a short space of time. Sadly, the situation continues because the authorities have refused to confront the issue.

The health of a church may also be evaluated by the way it is perceived by those outside in the community. Is the church focused inwards or directed outwards? Is it pastoral or evangelistic or both? Is it fired by a sense of mission or is it a country club?

Clearing the debris

Discernment is essential. Wink says that the angel of the church can become infected or demonic when the congregation turns its back on the specific tasks to which God has called it, or when it makes some other goal its idol. It may have become proud, arrogant or blinded by materialism, and may have lost its first love. Yet however far a congregation has deviated from God's will, the knowledge of that will is still encoded in the angel. Real change can only come as the spirit, the core essence of the whole congregation, is addressed and brought to transformation by Jesus, whose living word can transform us.

I remember a vivid experience of this one Friday, when I was walking in the park trying to discern and address the wounds in the church. I was due to preach on the church at Ephesus.[10] In preparation for the sermon I had read how the city of Ephesus was a mirror to the church: what had been happening in the city was a

10 See Revelation 2:1, 4–5, 'To the angel of the church of Ephesus write . . . You have forsaken your first love. Remember the height from which you have fallen! Repent and do the things you did at first.'

mirror of what was happening in the church. It is likely that John was using an important current event in the life of Ephesus as a basis for his imagery.

The coastline of Ephesus was continually changing because of the sediment brought down by the nearby River Cayster. Sand and pebbles progressively filled up the harbour, threatening to turn it into a swamp. The city was in danger of being moved out of its place, completely cut off from the sea. Two centuries earlier, a massive engineering project had dredged the harbour at the cost of much hardship. By the middle of the first century AD, however, the harbour was filling up with silt once again. It became apparent that if Ephesus was to retain her influence as a seaport the citizens would have to repent of their negligence and do the works they did at first. In AD 64 they began to dredge the harbour and Ephesus remained in its place for years to come. Over later centuries, silt was allowed to build up again. Now the sea is six miles away from the ruins of Ephesus. What was once the harbour is now a grassy, windswept plain.

As I mused on this, I tried hard to pray and discern what God was saying to us at St John's. Then, while I was walking through the park, I saw a large council sign by the lake:

DE-SILTING PROCESS
Due to de-oxidization of the water, a de-silting of the lake is in process so as to support plant life and fish in the lake.

In the lake was a large dredger, pumping sludge down the hill into an excavated pit. I went up to speak to one of the council workers. 'Has this been done before?' I asked.

'No,' he said, 'not that I know of.'

'Do you know how old the lake is?'

'About 80 years old.'

In that moment I knew that God had given me insight into the situation at St John's. Over the years the church had got silted up with all sorts of debris. Repentance and forgiveness was God's de-silting process that could free the church and give it oxygen that would support new life. God was asking us to deal with our painful memories as a church, not to allow the church to silt up and eventually die. That Sunday, as I related this experience, people's hearts were touched and they were able to respond in an act of repentance both for themselves as individuals and for the church that had become silted up.

The place of the prophetic

Over the following months we continued to seek God's vision and blessing for the church, and many people were praying. The gift of prophecy grew in the church, and one or two sensed that they were hearing God.

As I continued to read Revelation 2–3, I saw the place of the prophetic in unlocking the church from bondages and releasing new life. These letters are Christ's love initiative to the church to warn and woo her into a place of blessing and fruitfulness. They reveal the important role of the prophetic through which God can speak accurately to his church. The prophetic is the eyes and ears of the church – the ability to see and hear what the Spirit is saying to the church. Each of the seven churches in Revelation is different, but each prophecy gives an accurate assessment of where that church is and the potential of life for those who hear and act. To neglect what the

church in the locality of St John's. After my arrival I met with the house church leader, Nick Cuthbert, and Chris Turner, the Vicar of St Stephen's, Selly Oak, hoping to deal with our separatism and competition. We agreed to hold a joint service of our three churches at a local leisure centre, to confess and repent of our independence and seek to bless and honour each other's churches and ministries. That joint service grew to include 15 churches in south Birmingham and led to the 'Together For Birmingham' (TFB) initiative, an association of 80 ministers who met to pray for the city at Swanwick in January 1994.

We had also sensed that our attitude of pride and independence might be more deeply rooted than we originally thought. We were deeply influenced by our history. St John's Church had been carved out of the old parish of St Peter's. It was formed with a strong Protestant tradition, and had sent a number of letters to Parliament and to the Archbishop of Canterbury about maintaining the Church of England's Protestant tradition in its appointment of bishops and keeping true to its scriptural traditions. The church had also deplored the reintroduction of Mass vestments, after their disuse for three centuries, had protested against the introduction of the word 'altar', and had opposed any links with Rome indicated by the appointment of a British representative to the Vatican. It had also opposed changes in the Communion service, fearing this would sanction the gravest errors repudiated at the Reformation.[14]

This championing of truth can sometimes blind us to

---

14 PCC minutes of St John's, Harborne, 24th April 1904, 21st April 1911, 27th April 1916, 3rd April 1918.

the whole picture and give birth to an arrogant attitude, rooted in pride. We believed we needed to acknowledge both the good and the bad features of our forebears. As a result I went with our wardens to meet with the incumbent of St Peter's and his wardens, to thank them for planting St John's and to repent of any attitude of pride and independence which had infected relationships between our churches. We were keen to ensure that any roots were dealt with in a positive and constructive way that would ensure good relationships in the future.[15]

I see the nature of that first prophecy as corrective, but filled with hope. This fulfils the criteria Paul gives for true prophecy: 'But everyone who prophesies speaks to men for their strengthening, encouragement and comfort' (1 Corinthians 14:3). The gift of prophecy is releasing, because it gives us light to walk in, showing us what we need to take responsibility for, in order to bring about change.

The second prophecy highlighted a twofold idolatry that was infecting our church – materialism and rationalism. In St John's case, the materialism was all about comfortableness; the rationalism concerned the dominance of the mind. Part of the prophecy read as follows:

I felt in our rationalism, which is the backcloth to our Western way of life, we deny the power of God; but the poor and needy are desperate for the knowledge of a God of power, who can intervene and mend broken lives. We may feel we don't need miracles to convince of God's

15 See Hebrews 12:12, '"Make level paths for your feet," so that the lame may not be disabled, but rather healed.'

saving power but the lives of those outside are so messed
up, only a visible demonstration of God's power is going to
touch them; only a miraculous intervention will change
hopeless situations. We cannot limit God, the idol of rationalism does this, and it confines his working to what can be
understood by man.

Sharing the prophecy, Chris felt that these two idols had
afflicted the church for a long time, and in particular the
idol of rationalism. This resonated with a prosperous
church full of professionals, who were finding it difficult
to accommodate a supernatural worldview.

The third prophecy, given by Michael Harper, also
addressed issues that the church needed to face, but it
offered at the same time the promise of blessing and
hope for the future, if we acted on those issues.

Hear the word of the Lord: Take courage, I am with you.
Don't say within yourselves that this work is just a small
work; for I say to you, my people, that the splendour of this
house is mine, the silver and the gold is mine, everything
in the earth is mine. Begin to build again – stand on the
promises of God and the written word of God, be encouraged by the prophetic word as it comes forth.

I am with you, my people, I want to stir up your spirits
to believe that I am able to do beyond anything that you
have ever asked. I am always greater than your greatest
prayer; I am always greater than your highest aspiration.
Your praises are never greater than myself – and I want
you to magnify my name, I want you to exalt my name. I
want you to have faith tonight. I want you to be encouraged tonight. I want you to know that as you yield
yourselves to me, as you build in your personal lives an
altar unto the Lord, I will come down with fire on that

altar, and I will burn up all the dross, and all that is sinful and proud, and all that is mean and insignificant. And I will purge you, my people, and I will make you into a new people, and I will clothe you with my righteousness.

And I say to my people – take courage, for I am going to fill your house with my splendour. And I am going to take away from your lives that which has been waste, and that which has been unfruitful, that which has been purposeless. And in its place I am going to fulfil my purposes. For I am the Lord your God, I am the God of St John's, Harborne. Take courage my people. Surrender your timidity, surrender your doubts, surrender your fears, surrender your discouragements, and surrender your disillusionments. Surrender to me my people, lay your lives upon the altar. I shall be unto you your God, and I am even this night stirring up your spirit as I stirred up the spirit of Zerubbabel and the leaders in Jerusalem – so I am stirring you.

And do not busy yourselves with your own houses and your own affairs, and concern yourself overmuch with what is going to pass away – that which is as nothing in the balances.

And do not say in your heart, 'The time has not yet come.' For surely I have laid this thing upon you, and surely I have said to you, 'It shall be done.' The problem is not that you haven't heard my word but that you haven't obeyed it. You have not come and you have not done as I have told you. Repent, my people, for the time has come to begin to build it, and build in my strength, and with the courage that I give.

After we had explained the substance of these prophecies to the congregation at the meeting in December 1994, we asked those present to reflect on what they had heard and read, and to talk and pray about the prophecies in their small groups. There was a real spirit of prayer and repentance. I believe that was a very significant evening – the first time, to my knowledge, that the church had been called to weigh the gift of prophecies.

Since that time, we have increasingly realized what a gift prophecy is to the church. It allows us to see and respond to truth, to discern falsehood and turn from it. It also provides a key to intercession, for prophecy is conditional. It contains both warning and promise. The warning calls us to take responsibility for our actions and turn afresh to Christ. The promise needs to be grasped and prayed into the congregation's life.

Struggle and growth

This journey has been one of personal struggle, yet also one of growth. Sometimes my insecurity has been exposed in the face of criticism and has caused me to miss what people have really been saying. One leader said, 'John, sometimes we have missed each other.' That struck home. It led to discussions about how people perceived me as their pastor, and what I needed to do about that.

Leadership in a large church requires delegation of responsibilities and ministries, but oversight of the whole structure and maintenance of close relationships with key leaders. This managerial role was not one for which I was trained, and often my own particular pastoral responsibilities have been delegated because I needed to stand back and see the big picture. At other times, when there seemed to be a distrust or questioning of my leadership, I have wondered whether I am the right kind of leader for the church. I have needed support and encouragement to grow into rather than draw back from leadership. The words given to Gideon have been important to me: 'Go in the strength you have and save . . . Am not I sending you?' (Judges 6:14).

Two key leaders came to me one day to say that they wanted particularly to pray for and support me. That prayer triplet has been a source of strength, wise counsel and mutual encouragement ever since. It has given opportunity for growth, as well as a chance to talk through issues with a spiritual director. I believe strongly that the situation to which God calls us is tailor-made for our growth, but that growth demands that we face the issues and find God's grace in them.

The insights I have offered in this chapter, learned over a number of years, have been important to us as a church in the process of recovering our breath and our balance. They have also been valuable in our ministry to other churches engaged in the same process. In the next chapter I will look specifically at how we have dealt with areas of abuse – both in churches at which I have served as minister and in churches with which I have been involved in other ways.

9

Healing the Abuse and Hurts of the Church

Many churches have had to handle abuse that has taken place at the hands of either clergy or laypeople. Sometimes children are involved and whenever this is the case, under criminal law such matters must be taken up immediately with the denomination. In the Church of England this means going to the diocese through the archdeacon, after which the bishop's child protection adviser will investigate. No one can expect protection from the church authorities if children have been abused in any way.

Abuse is much more common than one might imagine, and it leaves some serious marks on the church involved, often hindering it in its progress. When a church is dying or failing to move forward, there is often some unresolved problem, either in the church itself or in the community, which affects the church's health. God is holy, and he cannot dwell in the midst of darkness. 'Your eyes are too pure to look on evil; you cannot tolerate wrong' (Habakkuk 1:13). If we do not face sin and repent, God will withdraw his hand from the church.

The kingdom advance is often arrested through the temptations of money, sex and/or power in the leadership of the church, be that the pastor or other significant leaders who have spiritual authority. We live in an age where many public leaders believe that what they do in private is no one else's business and has no bearing on their ability in public life. There is a divorce between personal and public morals. The Bible, however, will not countenance such a divorce. What we are in secret is what we are in the public arena. If I cannot be faithful to my wife and family, how can others trust me? What I am at the core will emerge in public, and an apple that is rotten at the core is a bad apple to eat.

There are two crucial keys to healing the church of any such wrongs, and these are also keys to healing a nation of its past evils. These keys are *corporate repentance* and *identificational repentance*. They have been principles of reconciliation in South Africa, Ireland and many other parts of the world. The church, however, has often been slow to use these keys and as a result has struggled with its legacy of wrongs.

Having said that, the concepts of corporate and identificational repentance have sometimes been used effectively by church leaders. The Pope, for example, has apologized to the Jews for the mistakes and sins of the past, and the Archbishop of Canterbury has apologized to Ireland for the sins of the English towards the Irish during and after the potato famine. Such acknowledgement of corporate responsibility is a necessary part of bringing about healing and reconciliation at all levels.

Similarly, in the political realm, secular leaders with God-given authority have acknowledged the wrongs of the past and made a public confession of that fact.

President Richard Freiherr von Weizsäcker, president of the Federal Republic of Germany, spoke to the Bundestag on the 8th May 1995. He talked of the knowledge that all Germans knew something terrible was happening to the Jews, and of the guilt that all Germans carried:

> Yet their forefathers have bequeathed on them a heavy legacy, and all of us, whether guilty or not, whether old or young, must accept the past. We must accept it by remembering it and not forgetting it. Whoever closes his eyes to the past becomes blind to the present. Whoever does not wish to remember inhumanity becomes susceptible to the dangers of a new infection.[1]

As president, Weizsäcker spoke for all of Germany, acknowledging that country's corporate guilt. The leader has a God-given responsibility to express on behalf of the nation what needs to be said. Failure to acknowledge corporate guilt means that difficult issues are swept under the carpet, only for them to flare up suddenly in the future. Such a failure was illustrated in Europe a few years ago in the Serb–Croat conflict. The tragedy there had its roots in the Second World War, in a concentration camp called Jasenovac where between 250,000 and 300,000 Serbs were exterminated by the Croatians. No attempt was made to deal with that past, with the result that Serbs and Croats still relive it today. The past cannot simply be brushed aside; reconciliation or healing begins when people deal with the past rather than ignoring it or trying to conceal it.

---

1   Quoted in Donald W. Shriver Jr, *An Ethic for Enemies: Forgiveness in Politics* (Oxford University Press, 1995), p. 110.

Corporate confession and repentance

We have lost the Hebrew concept of the corporate, and an understanding of the effect we have on one another's lives. The principle of the corporate – and particularly corporate sin – is crucial to an understanding of healing in the church. Following the Reformation this principle was one of the losses to the church in a reaction to some of the abuses of the priesthood and the system of indulgences.

The principle of 'justification by faith' that Luther enunciated so clearly was a gain, of course, but it played its part in the emergence of individualism that has been a foundation of Western society. The revival of interest in Greek philosophy during the seventeenth and eighteenth centuries produced the Enlightenment, or 'the age of reason' as it is commonly known. Modernity generated many of the ideas that shaped free-market capitalism, individual property rights and Western democracy. The Reformation restored to us the concepts of personal faith and individual salvation, but it seriously eroded the concept of the corporate that was so central to the worldview of the writers of the Old and New Testaments.

This concept is crucial to being church, in that any group of people will amount to more than the sum total of its individual members. Each church community has characteristics that were formed by those who founded the church and those who belonged to it in the past, influencing it for good or evil on its journey. The present members also affect it, by the attitudes and experiences of life they bring and the way they relate to one another. These factors are not impossible to change, but they do seem to have enduring effects, both past and present, and are not easily shifted.

The Bible gives many examples of the corporate being accepted as fact. The prophets address Israel as a corporate entity, bringing words of encouragement, warning and judgement, and calling for repentance from cities, peoples and nations. There are many prayers of confession that are spoken for generational, corporate and national sin by priests, prophets and civil leaders. One very familiar example is Solomon's prayer of dedication for the Temple.

> If my people, who are called by my name, will humble themselves and pray and seek my face and turn from their wicked ways, then will I hear from heaven and will forgive their sin and will heal their land. (2 Chronicles 7:14)

The word of God has many corporate categories: 'my people', 'themselves', 'their wicked ways', 'their sin', 'their land'. The idea is that the entire community was held responsible rather than a few deviant members.

Another example can be found in Joshua, when Achan's sin of taking the devoted things leads to Joshua's defeat at Ai. Joshua comes before the Lord mortified at the defeat and accuses God of letting him and his people down. 'Ah, Sovereign LORD, why did you ever bring this people across the Jordan to deliver us into the hands of the Amorites to destroy us?' (Joshua 7:7).

The New Testament also has examples of this worldview. Jesus affirms it in his intercession for the city of Jerusalem:

O Jerusalem, Jerusalem, you who kill the prophets and stone those sent to you, how often I have longed to gather your children together, as a hen gathers her chicks under her wings, but you were not willing. (Matthew 23:37)

The Old Testament scholar Gary Greig says, 'There is simply no New Testament evidence that suggests that either the Old Testament concept of generational sin or its corollary concept of confessing corporate, generational and national sin was negated in New Testament faith.'[2]

We see that concept again in Paul's first letter to the Corinthian church, when he addresses the issue of division marked at the Lord's Supper. The church's greed and neglect of the poor is affecting the corporate life of the church, bringing judgement, sickness and death. They have lost sight of their corporateness and are failing to discern the Lord's body (1 Corinthians 11:29–30).

Paul also writes of the dynamic of judgement, because sexual immorality is infecting the church. A man is having sex with his father's wife, his stepmother, and this is not being dealt with by the church. Paul accuses the church of being puffed up with pride since it has allowed such a thing to continue and its members are not filled with grief and have not put the man out of the fellowship. His judgement is that they are to 'hand this man over to Satan' (1 Corinthians 5:5). Discipline is necessary to deal with the sin, in order that his spirit might be saved. This action is not Paul's alone, but rather a community action, carried out in the context of

2 Gary Greig, 'A Biblical Basis for Identificational Repentance', published on the Internet at www.reconcile.org

the Spirit. Paul's word of prophetic judgement is to be heard and acted on by the whole church.

> The whole community must carry out this action, because the 'leaven' has affected them as a community: and as a community of the Spirit they must act in accordance with the Spirit's direction that has now been given them through Paul.[3]

The purpose of this judgement is to turn the sinner back out into Satan's sphere. That sphere contrasts to the gathered community of believers, where the Spirit is visibly manifest in the release of the gifts of the Spirit and loving concern for one another. This man is to be expelled into the world, where the evil one and his principalities and powers hold sway over people's lives to destroy them. These verses illustrate Paul's awareness of the danger of unconfessed sin, both to the sinner and to the church community. To overlook such sin is to open the church to the enemy's designs and to give ground to Satan.

One of the clearest examples of corporate sin in the whole Bible is the story of David dealing with the past in 2 Samuel 21. The issue is a past sin that Saul inflicted on the Gibeonites when he broke covenant with them. This was brought to David's attention through a famine that lasted three years, but David did not discern the truth very quickly. Sometimes the unravelling of the past will take time before we become aware that God is speaking. God's way of dealing with the past may be a process of unravelling first one thing, then another. In

---

3   Gordon Fee, *God's Empowering Presence* (Paternoster, 1995), p. 126.

my own experience, such unravelling is never a quick process, but it needs to be completed with due care.

With his kingdom beset by famine, David sought the face of the Lord, and the Lord spoke to him: 'It is on account of Saul and his blood-stained house; it is because he put the Gibeonites to death' (2 Samuel 21:1). David could have ignored this and settled for famine, but he chose to put things right. He called the Gibeonites to him and spoke to them. Israel had sworn to spare them (Joshua 9:15), but Saul in his zeal had tried to annihilate them. David asked the Gibeonites, 'What shall I do for you? How shall I make amends so that you will bless the LORD's inheritance?' (2 Samuel 21:3). They asked for seven descendants of Saul to be handed over and killed by them. In this way the blood-guilt was avenged. The principle illustrated the interplay between the corporate and the individual, and the retrospective nature of healing the past by means of an individual in leadership being willing to see the matter through.

Identificational repentance

If the acknowledgement of corporate sin is the first key to the healing of the church, the second is the principle of identificational repentance, as a means of averting God's judgement and bringing his mercy, release and healing from past sin.[4] Biblically, sin is dealt with through confession and repentance. The Bible is full of examples of leaders who not only confess personal sins

4 See Chris Seaton, 'Repenting for Others – A Paper Addressing Institutional and Generational Sin' (June, 2001).

but also identify themselves with the sins of the fathers, confessing them and asking for God's mercy. God promised:

> But if they will confess their sins and the sins of their fathers – their treachery against me and their hostility towards me, which made me hostile towards them so that I sent them into the land of their enemies – then when their ... hearts are humbled ... I will remember my covenant ... and I will remember the land. (Leviticus 27:40–42)

A clear example of such corporate and identificational confession comes in the book of Daniel. The exile was a judgement on Israel's disobedience. Jeremiah enunciates this consistently in his messages to Israel. After many warnings he declares God's judgement in the exile, which will be for 70 years (Jeremiah 25:7–14). This exile was to be a pivotal point in Israel's history, teaching them some fundamental truths about the nature of God and their mission to the world. They experienced God's goodness in the exile and the power of God's sovereignty acting on their behalf through a godly leader. They also learned to pray for the prosperity of the nation in which they were placed and to bring influence upon it.

Daniel understood from the Scriptures, particularly from Jeremiah, how long the exile would last. From that point he began to pray to the Lord and pleaded with him in sackcloth and ashes (Daniel 9:2–3). Daniel was a leader who identified with the sin of his fathers and prayed with repentance:

O Lord, the great and awesome God, who keeps his
covenant of love with all who love him and obey his commands, we have sinned and done wrong. We have been
wicked and have rebelled; we have turned away from your
commands and laws. We have not listened to your servants
the prophets, who spoke in your name to our kings, our
princes and our fathers, and to all the people of the land.
(Daniel 9:4–6)

In that prayer, Daniel identifies himself with the sin of
the fathers as though it was his own, and repents. He
honours God in his judgements, which are fully
deserved, and pleads for God's mercy and restoration.
The Lord hears Daniel's prayer and answers it in the
return of Ezra and Nehemiah, who go back to Jerusalem
to rebuild the Temple and the walls of the city. Both Ezra
and Nehemiah take on the identificational role of
repenting for the sins of the fathers (see Ezra 9:6;
Nehemiah 1:6–8).

The effect of the leaders' confession for themselves,
their forebears and all the people is to open the way for
the people to move into repentance for themselves. Such
a confession can unblock a log-jam and enable others to
move into the stream of corporate repentance. A leader
often starts this process, which is what we see happening with figures such as Ezra, Nehemiah, Daniel and
Jesus himself. Later in Ezra the people are able to
respond in confession and repentance for breaking the
covenant of marriage (Ezra 10). In Nehemiah, when the
people hear the reading of God's word they stand weeping before the Lord (Nehemiah 9).

The act of repentance by leaders on behalf of people
or by individuals on behalf of their families often

prepares the way for God to bring release into communities or families. This understanding gives us a key to cleansing, forgiving, releasing and healing the effects of the past on both people and land. There is a significant connection between the two. Our obedience brings blessing; our disobedience brings a curse on both people and land (Deuteronomy 28). It is, however, often also true that if the repentance is not followed through, a release is not forthcoming and stalemate occurs.

Some might say that, while the principle of identificational repentance was true in the Old Testament, it is not so clear that it was also true in the New Testament. I think this point can be answered in two ways. First, the members of the early church were birthed in the Jewish faith and were therefore deeply influenced by the fact of corporate repentance. When Paul says, 'All Scripture is God-breathed and is useful for teaching, rebuking, correcting and training in righteousness' (2 Timothy 3:16), he is speaking of the Old Testament documents. The church only formulated the New Testament documents later in the first century.

Second, we have the fact of Jesus' incarnation and identification with us as sinners. Jesus submitted to baptism by John, though John was reluctant to do it. Jesus said, 'Let it be so now; it is proper for us to do this to fulfil all righteousness' (Matthew 3:15). The Gospel informs us that Jesus was baptized into repentance. From this point his whole life was a statement of repentance, as he lived a life of obedience and offered what the first Adam failed to offer. It was because Jesus identified with us in becoming sin for us that his offering of obedience could be made in our place. That baptism of repentance was fulfilled at the cross. He hung on the cross as a representative person bearing the judgement that sin deserves, fully identified with us, yet offering his perfect obedience to God.

Jesus is the consummate example of a human being offering repentance to God on our behalf, for our sins and the sins of our fathers. God hears his prayers and releases his mercy and healing through him. This is the fulfilment of Peter's words, 'He himself bore our sins in his body on the tree, so that we might die to sins and live for righteousness; by his wounds you have been healed' (1 Peter 2:24).

Healing pain at St John's

Having outlined the two keys of corporate and identificational repentance, I believe it may be helpful to offer examples of how we used these keys at St John's to bring release and healing from the past.

As time passed, we noticed a sense of heaviness, sadness and isolation among God's people at St John's, and we never seemed to see things really moving forward unhindered. There appeared to be something that was resisting the Spirit's free flow in the church and all our activities.

A group of intercessors began to meet weekly to pray. This group came with no agenda except to seek the Lord and to pray as the Holy Spirit directed. Over the course of five years, they began to engage in powerful prayer with a sense of God's leading and a deep openness and trust in one another. They gave time to waiting on God, and God began to reveal things to them. I believe God gave them the spirit of intercession that has been so significant in our journey forwards. Intercession is a gift of

God through which he shares his heart and his longings about the things he wants to bring into being. It is a means by which the Spirit stirs in God's people and awakens his church.

It is terribly important for the church's growth that pastors look for those with this gift of intercession, those who will give time to wait on God and share with the leadership what they sense God is saying. Some of the significant actions we have taken to deal with the past and to sense what God is after in the present have arisen from times of intercession.

I am particularly struck by a verse from Amos, when God shows the prophet what is going to happen to Jacob and he finds it too painful to contemplate. That pain is the birthplace of intercession. God also shows the prophet the complacency of his people, which offends him. 'You drink wine by the bowlful and use the finest lotions, but you do not grieve over the ruin of Joseph' (Amos 6:6). Grieving over sin and the complacency of the church is a gift that God gives, and where people respond to his Spirit, they will feel this sorrow and often react with tears. Many have experienced this gift in services or at home in their prayers. The history of the Orthodox Church also speaks much about the gift of tears.

On the first day of the new millennium I went down with a bad bout of flu and a severe cough, and I lost my voice for two months. I had an operation on my throat to check that nothing sinister was lurking on my vocal chords. There was a swelling and a biopsy was needed to eliminate any suspicion. I was exhausted because of the flu, and found myself struggling with depression. For two months, I was not allowed to speak.

The prayer group were aware not only of the possibility

of me losing my voice temporarily, but also of the danger of me being silenced in a more lasting way. If the voice damage was permanent, there was a possibility that I would not be able to continue in ministry. Bob Dunnett came to visit me and shared his belief that we were in the midst of a considerable spiritual battle, and that I was under attack. This resonated with me because in one sense I had been 'gagged' through the loss of my voice. The group continued to pray into this, and over the next few weeks it came to light that there had been some sexual and physical abuse that had taken place in the church many years previously. Obviously for reasons of confidentiality I cannot be specific, suffice to say it was serious and involved a number of people.

I had possessed some knowledge of these occurrences for some time, but not the full extent, and had been waiting for further confirmations and substantiation.[5] A number in the church had been aware of some 'stronghold' that had been a block to the church's blessing and freedom, and with the facts I now had I needed to know God's wisdom as to how to deal with this matter. Obviously this needed complete confidentiality. Equally, the church needed to be set free from the painful memories of the past, and the bondage these had brought into the church's spiritual life. It had become clear that the secrecy and 'gagging' needed to be broken and the truth should come into God's light. We are seeing in these days that the abuse of the past is coming into the open and people who have wronged and abused children are being held accountable.

---

5 See 1 Timothy 5:19, 'Do not entertain an accusation against an
   elder unless it is brought by two or three witnesses.'

Lessons from South Africa

It is interesting to step aside from the story for a moment and note the part played by the Truth and Reconciliation Commission in South Africa in the effort to unlock that country from its past. I spent a sabbatical in South Africa during February and March 1999, studying the workings of the TRC. The experience had a profound effect on me, and influenced the way I was to handle the difficult situation back home at St John's.

The TRC amnesty hearings were based on a Christian ideal inspired by Archbishop Desmond Tutu. His belief was that the truth needed to come out into the open, so that the bereaved could know what had happened to their loved ones who were murdered by the state. This was of paramount importance, because those who had been arrested and tortured were told, 'Go ahead, scream as much as you like, no one hears you and no one will ever know.' The hearings exposed the lie of silence and restored the strength of human dignity to victims, who could now tell their story knowing that an attentive commission listened and believed. They also heard what happened to lost loved ones, and hearing that truth helped them to move forward.

There were some astonishing stories of forgiveness and reconciliation, although not all could make that journey. What has become patently obvious, however, is that truth-telling liberates people from the past, while concealing things destroys true relationship. This background knowledge of how the past could be unlocked became a helpful model for us to follow at St John's.

The common factors of all processes of reconciliation in major religious traditions are, first, that the wrongdoing is acknowledged; second, that there is some form of atonement, perhaps in the form of a service or symbol; third, that the perpetrator resolves to make apology and not repeat the offence; and fourthly, that reparations are made where possible. The process may not always be possible to complete, because it is dependent upon the individual parties involved, but those are the elements necessary to make a way forward.

Facing the issues

I bore these lessons carefully in mind when it came to dealing with the issue of abuse at St John's in order to bring healing. First of all, I called a small group of leaders together to tell them what I had discovered, assuring them that people in the church and further afield had confirmed the facts. I read out a precise account of what had taken place. The veil of secrecy needed to be broken and the truth known by others, for it was bigger than I could handle. It was also true that we needed a small group who could represent the church and move together in a process of corporate repentance.

Some members of the group were more deeply scarred by the occurrences, so I met with them on a further occasion to deal with their painful memories. I asked a clergyman and his wife to come in to listen to the stories, to lead a Communion and to pray for the individuals. Each person was given time to speak what was on their heart and were able to express fully the hurt, pain and disappointment. They were listened to without interruption. We took time to pray over them for release and healing, and then we completed the process with a Eucharist. We all felt that we had faced up to the issue and repented, and that the whole matter was now placed before God for his mercy and healing. It was like lancing an abscess, drawing out the poison and applying a healing ointment. The conspiracy of silence had been broken, and the truth had set people free (John 8:32).

Following that occasion, I met with a larger group in the context of a Eucharist. We came together to pray on behalf of the church, to repent and ask God's mercy for what had taken place. I used some stones as a symbol of the weight this had left on the church.

I was very struck at the time with the Lectionary readings from Daniel: Daniel took corporate responsibility for confessing the sins of the nation that led to the exile, and he prayed a prayer of identificational repentance. He said, 'We have not sought the favour of the LORD our God by turning from our sins and giving attention to your truth' (Daniel 9:13). Sometimes we can forgo the favour of God by being more afraid to upset people than to face what is happening and address it. I wonder if, behind many churches' lack of progress there lies unresolved conflict or sin that has not been repented of and addressed. Facing it might cause disturbance, but that can lead to resolution, which is far better than being locked in the past.

At the Eucharist service, each person in the group held a stone as we entered a time of confession and repentance. We completed that time by placing the stones in a semicircle on the floor. We then used other stones to symbolize the abusers, and put them into the hands of God. We prayed further for healing and blessing for the church, and waited on God. We received some very encouraging words of Scripture and prophecy.

The fruit of this prayer was not long in coming. Many people felt that something had been broken and there seemed to be a new freedom in the church and in me, their minister. At Pentecost we experienced a release of God's Spirit among us and that sense of God's blessing seems to be continuing. It is as though a weight has been lifted from the church and a new thing is happening. I have recovered my voice now and sense a new lightness in my ministry.

Sharing responsibility

Where a disturbance of some kind has taken place, it seems terribly important that it should not be swept under the carpet, but should be dealt with confidentially in some way, so that an unlocking can take place and the church can be freed to move forward from its past. As clergy, we are under the pastoral authority of our bishop, who shares the cure of souls with us. Where something has been covered up in the past that is later substantiated, it is right to share the facts with the bishop, who can offer guiding counsel. The bishop should certainly be forewarned of the situation in case it should become public, but it is also helpful that he is detached from the situation and can therefore provide an objective assessment. There is also strength to be gained from sharing the weight of responsibility.

I have been privileged to go to many churches to take weekends or talk with leaders about where the church has been arrested in its progress. Sadly, it has become common for ministries to be shipwrecked through those three principal areas of money, sex and power. The fall of a minister leaves a church wounded and the fabric of relationships and trust broken. Often the difficult issues are not faced and dealt with, leaving the church to limp along and robbing it of the cleansing and healing process.

I remember a church where the vicar and curate were both involved in adulterous affairs in the parish, and both resignations were announced on the same Sunday. The parish was shaken by the news and needed help to work through their grief and sense of betrayal. The realization that a pastor has feet of clay is often painful and disappointing for many. That sense of pain is a profound experience and needs to be given a place for expression. The church needs to come into a place of openness where people can express their disappointment and shame and forgive their leader, so that a distrust of leadership may not become a block to the future. If people face the truth and come in repentance, God in his mercy may redeem that church and unlock a new future. This reflects very powerfully the gospel of the second chance.

It will, of course, take time for a community to rebuild trust in a new leader, and he or she needs to be sensitive to that fact. The church is making a journey towards healing from its painful past. That past experience can be faced corporately by the whole church if all the information is in the public domain, or by a representative group if the facts are still confidential. Such a representative group can then pray corporately on behalf of the church. Whatever the situation, time will be needed for the process to be completed.

Counselling

A colleague at St John's was due to move on to take up the post of team vicar in a church where the previous leader had to relinquish his position because he had gone off with the churchwarden's wife, leaving two broken families. As my colleague and I reflected on this before he left St John's, we recognized the need to give time for the healing process. We also saw the need to be careful in any pastoral work which involved a man seeing women alone. Such meetings should be conducted in the presence of another person, if possible the pastor's own wife. We understood that there was an urgent need to model the strength of marriage in that community, both by sharing the work and by promoting family in the church.

Counselling members of the opposite sex demands great care. Deep spiritual awareness and attachments can grow apparently innocently, but can become a danger. There is a great joy to be found in corporate prayer and in seeing God work to release an individual, and that joy creates a bond between you and the person with whom you have been praying. Without due care, this could lead to a growing and inappropriate attachment.

When I pray with someone in counselling, I only do so if that person is happy to allow a third person to join us. I explain that Jesus sent the disciples out in twos, and we follow that pattern, to provide added faith, strength and wisdom and to deter any manipulation that might occur if one person only were involved. It also offers the chance to confer about the direction of the prayer ministry. We also follow this principle in the prayer ministry that takes place after our services, so that the ministry is seen as part of the corporate body and not the ministry of any individual. The other major reason for this practice is that it is a superb way of mentoring new people into ministry. Jesus followed this rabbinical method of developing ministry with his disciples:

- He did it before them and they watched (Mark 2–3).
- He did it with them and they participated (Matthew 14:13–33).
- He let them do it and dealt with feedback (Matthew 10:1–20; Mark 6:8–11; Luke 9:1–6; 10:1–24).
- He left them doing it, so the ministry increased and developed (Acts).

There is a marvellous phrase in Luke 24, on the walk to Emmaus, when Cleopas expresses his disappointment to Jesus: 'We had hoped that he was the one who was going to redeem Israel' (Luke 24:21). Disappointments and feelings are part of being human and need expression if we are to find release and come to a place of thanksgiving. God is always able to redeem the past, be that in an individual or in the corporate life of a church, but the reality is that the process is costly. It means facing the past and its pain, repenting and seeking where possible to take steps to put things right.

A walk of repentance

When I was in Port Elizabeth in South Africa, I met the Diocesan Bishop Eric Pike. He shared with me a wonderful example of corporate symbolic repentance, describing a 200-kilometre walk that he had completed during Lent. He believed God had prompted him to embark on that walk of reconciliation.

The idea came to him when he heard God speaking through an Indian priest, Cliff Felix, who said that before the diocese could move forward to transformation, they needed to 'lance the boil'. He asked Cliff to speak further about this, and realized that there was much pain in all the people of his diocese because of the hurts and guilt created by apartheid. The hurt and the guilt both needed to be dealt with. He set up a commission, which concluded that they needed a pilgrimage of cleansing. Apartheid had affected everyone in a different way – all were dehumanized to some extent, but many people had suffered very deeply. As a church we acknowledge the truth that 'if one part [of the body] suffers, every part suffers with it' (1 Corinthians 12:26). The commission came up with a report suggesting that anything undertaken in the diocese needed to include various elements:

- Confessions of our various failures as a church in opposing racism and apartheid and in supporting those most gravely disadvantaged by it.
- The acknowledgement that whilst there were many who resisted with great courage and suffering, nevertheless, all have something personally to confess for their part in supporting or acquiescing at times in the evil of apartheid. The people most disadvantaged by the system need to be able to regard themselves as 'survivors' not 'victims', and so become 'victors'.
- The need to equip clergy and laity to minister to the deep hurts of the past, as well as to help people to recognize the wrongs they have supported.
- To address the needs of reparation.

- To tangibly express hope for the future of our people and land and make a commitment to it.[6]

This led to two decisions. First, they planned to hold simultaneous, formal 'services of cleansing' in the eight archdeaconries of the diocese, each one to be held in a church that had suffered in the time of apartheid. The services were held on the 14th February 1999, with representatives of all communities taking part and collections going to a diocesan reparation fund.

Second, the bishop decided to embark on a ten-day walk during Lent that would symbolize 'presence, prayer and protest'. Bishop Pike's focus was threefold: (1) to make the presence of Jesus known to those who were bereaved and had suffered as a result of violence, and to be a visible presence to them; (2) to pray for the country and its people against the forces of darkness, and to pray for the light of Jesus to shine on them; (3) to make a statement of protest to the government for the inadequacies of the criminal justice system in dealing with the issue of violence.

Each evening he stopped at places where violence had occurred and where people had been murdered, and met with the bereaved families to listen to their stories, to pray for them and comfort them, and to pray over the places where the evil had happened. He held services of cleansing and healing, sometimes involving some 700 or more people. As he walked, he prayed for the brokenness of the country. He was often tempted to

6 Eric Pike, Bishop of Port Elizabeth, 'Report on the Healing of Hurts of Apartheid (Lance the Boil) Commission', 30th October 1997.

look back and see how far he had walked, but he received a clear message from God not to look back, but to look forward to the light ahead. He also realized how people from all communities were affected and the importance of walking across the racial divide. He encouraged people to unite and speak out against injustice, violence and crime.

There is much we could all learn from Eric's example about being intent to heal the past and to pay something of the cost to ensure that the pain is dealt with. Eric was often overwhelmed with tears as he met and stood with the people who had suffered – but he also brought immense comfort, for here was a leader who was listening to, empathizing with and praying for his people.

In a letter to the people of the diocese, Eric set down some reflections of his unique pilgrimage to places of murder, rape and violence.

I knew from the start that it would be asking much of the people who had suffered as a result of murder, rape and violent crimes committed against members of their respective families to visit with me the places of the crimes, but praise God they came. There were often tears, both theirs and mine, but God was present to heal and I felt something of the reality of the words of the prophet Jeremiah, who said, 'They treat the wounds of my people as if they were not serious.' How could I approach people who had suffered so much, and ask if I, a stranger, could pray for them, if I hadn't come on foot and in a small measure identified with their pain in seeking to express something, not only of the church's love and compassion, but also of our penitence before God for the sins of our land?[7]

7   Bishop Eric Pike, 'Reflections of a Pilgrim', March 1999.

I think this is a wonderful example of dealing with the past before God, corporately, with due care, attention and responsibility, helping to exorcise the scar that apartheid had over all the community, victims, perpetrators and those who kept silent. David Bosch from South Africa said this about forgiveness: 'Confessing our guilt is itself a supreme blessing and a sign of grace. It opens up the fountains of new life and cleanses us.'[8]

Guiding principles

In summary of this difficult subject, and to draw together some of the threads which have run through the previous few chapters, I would like to set out some guiding principles that can help in renewing and healing a church.

1. If you are moving to pastor a new church, know that God has called you to this place and desires to renew his church. Changeovers are always vulnerable times to both the church and the leader, as people become wedded to a particular leader who has been significant in their lives. We can see that God has this process clearly in control during the changeovers of leadership between Moses and Joshua, Elijah and Elisha, Saul and David, Paul and Timothy. Our vision, like God's, should not be static. A leader does not come to repeat the past, but to do a new thing. Churches need to welcome what is new as well as

---

8   Professor David Bosch, paper read on 11th September 1985 and reproduced in Klaus Nurnberger, *The Cost of Reconciliation in South Africa* (MPO, 1988) pp. 109–110.

incorporate what is old. The new leader will have a new style of doing things and a new way of seeing.

2. Listen to what God is saying and what he wants to do. Listening is vital. The church may be tired and may want to reflect on the past and learn God's way forward. I believe it is right that a new leader should trust his or her sense of what God may be saying, writing it down before he or she can rationalize that sense away. Often God will be giving you insight for the future that will be confirmed by others in the short term.

3. Welcome the ministry of the prophets. We came up to St John's with a sense of what God was saying as well as a specific prophetic word. These words need to be weighed and prayed over, but they can be very important in terms of giving direction to the church. We need also to be watchful of those who give directional prophecy to the church, ensuring that we know something of their character and standing.

4. Hear what God is saying to the angel of the church and the community (see pages 157–159). It is important to listen to the story of the church and the community's journey of faith, because this will often reveal much about the health of the church.

5. Heal the angel of the church by facing moments of failure and conflict through repentance and faith. This journey is not one to face alone. Work with the other leaders and those who have office in the church.

6. Provide opportunities for release and letting go. Often symbolism can be very helpful in this process (see pages 154–155).

7. Make a fresh structure for renewal. The past struc-

tures may be too rigid and may have become a monument to a blessing rather than a means of blessing. It may be wise to invite other churches to come over and give what they have been given: we must never make the mistake of believing that we have all that there is to have. Such pride will rob us of blessing. We need continually to be open to what God is doing. 'See, I am doing a new thing . . . do you not perceive it?' (Isaiah 43:19).

10
Healing and Deliverance

One cannot read the Gospels without realizing that the central message of Jesus is a proclamation of the kingdom. After his baptism he strode into Galilee proclaiming the good news of the kingdom. '"The time has come," he said. "The kingdom of God is near. Repent and believe the good news!"' (Mark 1:15). Jesus' kingdom message is very wide in its scope. It includes healing the sick, setting the captives free, righting economic priorities, seeking justice for the oppressed and confronting oppressive leaders, and restoring right relationships through forgiveness and reconciliation. It is corporate, economic, political, emotional, physical, psychological and personal in its breadth.

I believe it is extremely important not to limit our understanding of the ministry of healing, for it includes all that restores dignity to each human being. Jürgen Moltmann expressed this superbly when speaking about the breadth of healing.

There are also objective unjust circumstances which make people ill as social medicine has shown. So it is impossible to heal the sick without healing their relationships, the circumstances in which they live, and the social structures of the social system to which they belong. It therefore makes sense not to consider disease solely in the isolations of their pathogenic causes, but to see those who are ill in the context of their life history, and to view their life history as part of their social history.[1]

In Luke's Gospel, Jesus began his ministry by reading from Isaiah.

> The Spirit of the Lord is on me,
> because he has anointed me
> to preach good news to the poor.
> He has sent me to proclaim
> freedom for the prisoners
> and recovery of sight for the blind,
> to release the oppressed,
> to proclaim the year of the Lord's favour.
> (Luke 4:18–19; Isaiah 61:1–2)

Jesus then said, 'Today this scripture is fulfilled in your hearing' (Luke 4:21). He proceeded to teach and fulfil this word, by driving out evil and healing the sick. He called his disciples and taught them to proclaim the kingdom and to do the works of the kingdom. It was his intention to leave the disciples continuing both the word and the works of the kingdom. The Acts of the Apostles shows that this intention was fulfilled as the disciples, empowered by the Spirit, continued doing the work of healing and driving out demons.

---

1 J. Moltmann, *Power and the Powerless* (SCM Press, 1983).

Gifts for the present time

When I was at St Mark's Gillingham, our curate David Watson led a Bible study on the Holy Spirit for young leaders. His conclusion then was that the gifts of the Holy Spirit were meant only for the age of the apostles and were no longer needed by today's church. B. B. Warfield, articulating this doctrine of 'dispensationalism', argued that the purpose of the gifts was to authenticate the apostles as trustworthy teachers of doctrine. When they died, therefore the gifts 'necessarily passed away with them'. Warfield wrote in 1918,

> These gifts were not the possession of the primitive Christians as such: nor for that matter of the Apostolic age for themselves; they were distinctly for the authentication of the Apostles. They were part of the credentials of the Apostles as the authoritative agents of God in founding the church. Their function thus confined them to distinctively the Apostolic Church, and they necessarily passed away with it.[2]

Dr Jack Deere, however, gives a well-reasoned refutation of Warfield's doctrine in his book *Surprised by the Power of the Spirit*, and I think argues convincingly that dispensationalism is not a valid principle.[3]

A few months after that study on the Holy Spirit, at a night of prayer in February 1962, a whole group of us were filled with the Holy Spirit and began to experience

---

2 Benjamin B. Warfield, *Counterfeit Miracles* (Banner of Truth Trust, 1972), p. 6.

3 Jack Deere, *Surprised by the Power of the Spirit* (Hodder & Stoughton, 1994), pp. 57–76.

the gifts of the Spirit first hand. Our worldview had to change because what we had experienced challenged all our previous thinking. To put it another way, our paradigm had to change because we were dealing with a new reality that did not fit our previous grid.

A paradigm is an example or pattern. A shift indicates moving from one model or pattern to another. There is a well-known picture that illustrates how this works. The picture is of both a young lady and an old hag. Many cannot see both of them. The lines of the drawing do not shift, but there is a shift in the perception of the observer. As the observer looks at the picture, the visual patterns seem to shift. This, on a small scale, demonstrates how a paradigm shift or change of worldview works.

A further illustration of this truth can be seen in the diagram on page 205. I have found it to be very helpful in the way that it demonstrates how we can expect the kingdom of God to be breaking into the present. Whenever a healing, reconciliation, act of forgiveness or answer to prayer occurs, the future kingdom is breaking into the present.

The present age is under the power of the prince of this age – you might call it the realm of disobedience, or the kingdom of darkness. Through the commandments in the Bible we know what we are called to, but are unable to attain it because we have a bias towards sin. In order to enter the future age, the kingdom of light, we need a Saviour figure to deliver us from this present age and transfer us into the age to come. That is what God enabled when he sent his Son into the world, as Paul explains in Galatians 4.

> So also, when we were children, we were in slavery under the basic principles of the world. But when the time had fully come, God sent his Son, born of a woman, born under law, to redeem those under law, that we might receive the full rights of sons. (Galatians 4:3–5)

Jesus achieves that purpose through the incarnation, through becoming one with us, and through the cross he established a 'bridgehead' through which the future kingdom could break into the present. He rescued us from the dominion of darkness. Paul speaks of that transfer from the kingdom of darkness to the kingdom of light in Colossians: 'For he has rescued us from the dominion of darkness and brought us into the kingdom of the Son he loves, in whom we have redemption, the forgiveness of sins' (Colossians 1:13).

The cross earths the work of Jesus in history. Through the cross the cosmic powers of evil are broken, and through faith in God's redeeming work we are transferred into the kingdom of his beloved Son. In that kingdom, God's future is breaking into the present. We are a people who live in the overlap. We taste the powers to come, but that taste is only a firstfruit; it is not the fullness that is yet to come.

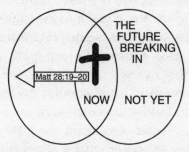

PRESENT AGE   FUTURE AGE

In the diagram, however, the cross is the bridgehead by which the future invades the present. The arrow pointing from the cross into the present symbolizes the advance of God's kingdom into our present world. Our activity seeks to advance the future kingdom into the present. Evangelism, faith-sharing, prayer, healing and deliverance are signs of the kingdom being manifested in the present. The Spirit of God is not absent from that circle, because he is everywhere, but his presence also needs particular expression. So when we pray, 'Your kingdom come on earth as it is in heaven', we are praying for the kingdom of God to advance in this present age. We look forward to a time when this world will be redeemed and will be full of the glory of God as the waters cover the sea. We enjoy now the firstfruits of what will fully come when Jesus returns.

> Not only so, but we ourselves, who have the firstfruits of the Spirit, groan inwardly as we wait eagerly for our adoption as sons, the redemption of our bodies. For in this hope we were saved. (Romans 8:23–24)

Living in tension

The New Testament teaches us that in the coming of Jesus the future age has come into the present; the kingdom of God has come but is not yet consummated. It is both present and future. We are part of both the 'already' and the 'not yet', and we have to learn to live with that tension. God gives enough evidence of Christ raised to call to faith, but not enough evidence to compel acceptance. Again and again the gifts of the Spirit operate, yet they are never wholly at our disposal. There remains something sovereign and elusive about their coming and going. In the realm of healing, much happens to authenticate Christ's present will and power to heal the otherwise incurable, and yet, often distressingly, enough fails to happen to remind us that we are not yet at the last day, leaving the mystery of the 'not yet' all around us.

It can be dangerous to loosen that tension in either direction. To put Christ's resurrection power exclusively into the future is to make him utterly remote and withdrawn from us, leaving us alone with our efforts and bereft of any participation in his gifts to us. On the other hand, to claim that completeness of resurrection is open to us here and now is to fall into a cruel charismatic triumphalism. This can lead us to refuse to accept our failures and to deceive others (and ourselves) into imagining that everything works out immediately and completely for those who are in the Spirit, that all the prophecies are fulfilled and all the sick are healed.

The truth is that we have to live in a far less simple situation than either of these scenarios – a situation in which the comfort of the here-and-now Spirit and the mystery of the not-yet Spirit constantly, and in the end creatively, confront us. Anyone who has been involved in the ministry of healing knows the pain and cost of walking this tightrope. They will know the difficulty of trying to work in a sensitive way that will not draw back from the risk of faith, but that will also avoid laying a heavier burden on those who hope for healing.

Our perception of the world

Before engaging with the practice of healing, I want to mention two important factors that influence our perspective of the healing ministry. The first factor concerns our perception of the world and the way it works. Earlier in the chapter I indicated that the way we see the world affects deeply what we anticipate and receive. We live in a secular society that has a different worldview from the New Testament, so there is often a conflict between our own thinking and the more primitive faith of the New Testament Christians. Our secular worldview omits the possibility of God acting in power to restore the sick. We live comfortably with medicine because it is a science of our age, but the idea of supernatural intervention is outside our comfort zone.

Charles Kraft, a missionary thinker, said in 1979:

> All of us have basic assumptions of how we view the world that are rooted in our culture. But other peoples of other cultures start from other assumptions and come out with very different conclusions. Their assumptions may be just as valid as ours, but focused on a part of the data we ignore.[4]

---

4 Charles H. Kraft, *Christianity in Culture* (Orbis Books, 1984), p. 52.

Dr Paul Hiebert, Professor of the School of World Missions at Fuller Seminary College and himself a missionary in India, says, 'The Western worldview has a blindspot that makes it very difficult for many Western missionaries and pastors to understand, let alone answer, problems related to spirits, ancestors and astrology.'[5]

In this context, Dr Hiebert has spoken about the uneasiness he experienced as a missionary in India. John's disciples asked Jesus, 'Are you the one who was to come, or should we expect someone else? (Luke 7:20). Jesus answered not by offering logical proofs, but by giving a demonstration of power as he cured the sick and cast out evil spirits. When Dr Hiebert read that passage in India, however, there was a strange uneasiness. As a Westerner he was used to presenting truth on the basis of rational arguments, not the evidence of power in the lives of people who were sick, possessed and destitute. The ministry of Christ in confronting evil spirits belonged in Hiebert's mind to a separate world of the miraculous, for which he had no framework. Now, however, his worldview came under challenge.

In India, if people were sick they had various categories of people to whom they could go for help. Life-threatening cases were taken to the *sadhu* – a saint. If they needed supernatural help, they went to a *mantrakar* – a magician. Other cases were taken to a doctor or a 'quack' who used folk remedies. Hiebert puzzled over the question of spirit possession, curses,

---

5 Paul Hiebert, 'The Flaw of the Excluded Middle', *Missiology: An International Review* (American Society of Missiology, January 1982), vol. 10, no. 1.

witchcraft and black magic. What was the Christian answer to these? He realized that his worldview was inadequate when it came to categorizing either the New Testament or the Indian worldview. His modern Western worldview excluded the supernatural – a central factor in both New Testament and Indian perceptions of the world.

As Westerners we are taught to deal with the empirical world in terms of observation and experience. As theologians we are taught to answer ultimate questions in theistic or otherworldly terms. For most of us, the 'middle zone' of the supernatural does not exist. We do not acknowledge that there may be supernatural forces at work on this earth. How did this happen? How did this change of mindset come about?

It was a growing acceptance of Platonic dualism in the seventeenth and eighteenth centuries that caused the belief in that middle zone to fade away. A new science based on materialistic naturalism emerged, which led to the secularization of science and the mystification of religion. Science worked in areas of experimentation that were provable, whereas religion was left to faith, visions, dreams and inner feelings. The whole realm of the supernatural was excluded because it was not provable in the accepted sense.

Today we are at last starting to take a different view, beginning once again to acknowledge a worldview that includes the middle zone, a theology which includes God working in human history and individual lives now. More specifically, the National Health Service in Britain is conducting pilot models in alternative medicine, and one forward-thinking GP is employing a chaplain who offers a prayer clinic. Birmingham

University is assessing that model and will report on it to the NHS. My wife Annie is the chaplain involved and has a specific responsibility for care of the dying, the prayer clinic and the staff team. This is a rare opening, however, and I have observed from my own experience as hospital chaplain the countless opportunities that doctors have at the sharp end of life, from which pastors are often excluded.

We need to recover a theology that is open to God interacting with his world, in providing for our needs, in healing, in delivering the oppressed. We have excluded God and his power from our theology, and thus from our churches. Fearing what we could not control or understand, we have thrown the baby out with the bath water. To exclude that middle zone, to exclude the possibility of God's power working in our world today, is to rob us of a framework which can help to bring the gospel to the whole person and to the whole of God's world.

Jesus has bidden us to pray the prayer of the kingdom, to pray for an increase of the kingdom to break into the present. Any answer to prayer is the future breaking into the present. Any healing or breaking of the powers of darkness in individual lives or communities is God's future becoming present here and now. The Spirit groans within us – there is a longing for the fullness that is coming. When we meet signs of the powers of darkness there is something within us that recognizes that this is not how things were intended to be. That groaning is a prayer of the kingdom at work within us.

The idea of the kingdom present and the kingdom coming speaks of a gap between the two ages. There is a battle to be fought by the church in this age, against an enemy who has been conquered but is still seeking to hold on to what he had. The devil seeks to obstruct in any way he can the advancing kingdom of God. We are at war with an enemy who holds people captive to this present age (see Ephesians 2:2).

The gap between the two ages might best be illustrated with an analogy from the Second World War. There was a significant gap of time between D-Day and VE Day. D-Day, the 6th June 1944, was the beginning of the end, the day when the Allies landed in northern France. That was the day when the war turned and victory was assured – but there was still much fighting to be done before that victory was completed. Likewise, in Jesus' incarnation, life of obedience, death on the cross, resurrection and ascension into heaven, the victory was assured – but the church must continue to fight from that place of assurance until the victory is completed. VE Day, the 8th May 1945, was the day fixed for the victory celebrations that marked the end of the hostilities in Europe. Likewise, the battle against Satan will be completed when Jesus returns and finally puts Satan under his feet and delivers the kingdom to his Father: 'Then the end will come, when he hands over the kingdom to God the Father after he has destroyed all dominion, authority and power. For he must reign until he has put all his enemies under his feet' (1 Corinthians 15:24–25).

If we are to engage in the ministry of healing and deliverance today, we will not do so consistently if we have a distorted worldview. We need to recover a New Testament perspective and gain an increasing confidence in God's power and God's victory. This is part of our calling as ministers of the gospel.

God's ministry

The second important factor to bear in mind is that the ministry of healing is God's ministry to those who are sick. Whether that ministry comes through medical aid or through prayer, it is God's gift to those who need it. There should be no division in our thinking on this matter. Christians should be thankful for the fullness of God's provision, and should live comfortably both with the work of the physicians and with the resources of the church's prayers. Sadly, such an inclusive view does not always prevail, and we need reminding that what God has joined together we should not divide. There is no distinction between healing through the skills of medicine and spiritual healing in the name of Christ. It is not that one is better or more God-given than the other; it is simply that the witness they bear is different.

Medical healing bears witness to the providence of God in creation, providing within the natural order remedies and human skills to cure the ills of his creatures. Divine healing, by contrast, bears witness to the operation of the Holy Spirit breaking through the limitations of the natural (as he did when he raised Christ from the dead). One gives testimony to a God who provides within creation; the other gives testimony to a risen Christ and to a God who can reverse the natural processes. Both are meant to live comfortably with one another. Both should give rise to thankfulness and gratitude towards God the provider.

I want to look at two stories in the New Testament – concerning the man with leprosy and the paralytic in Luke 5. Jesus indicates that there are three important factors in the healing ministry. First, God is active: 'the

power of the Lord was present . . . to heal' (Luke 5:17).
Jesus certainly recognized moments when that was true,
and multiple healings took place. Whether or not a part
was played in the process by a release of faith in the
people asking (which seems to be the case with the man
with leprosy), the important point to grasp is that the
healing is God's doing. It is initiated by his action in
response to the faith he has given, and has little to do
with our own striving or effort. It is God's power that
heals, not our human techniques or fervency in prayer.
Healing is a grace that God imparts.

Second, Jesus reveals God's willingness to heal; he
is not a reluctant giver. We will not easily embark on
the ministry of healing if in our hearts we believe
that God is reluctant to impart his touch on
people's lives. We need to get that issue settled
before we start out. The leper describes it perfectly:
'Lord, if you are willing, you can make me clean'
(Luke 5:12). He was certain that Jesus could heal him
if he chose to – his question centred on his willingness.
Jesus expressed the Father's heart, saying, 'I am willing
. . . Be clean!' (v. 13). Immediately the leprosy left
him. There is a great need in the church to see God as
he is, not through the spectacles of our scientific
rationalism, which diminishes any seed of faith.

Third, faith is a requirement that looks to God with
expectation. In both stories, faith shines through. The
faith of the leper means that he knows for certain that
Jesus is the Lord who can and will heal. Jesus sees a
faith that can receive the kingdom, and releases that into
the man's life. The faith of the four friends of the paral-
ysed man is a picture of the corporate church looking to
God with expectation on behalf of another whose faith

has all but dried up. Jesus responds to that corporate faith. 'Friend, your sins are forgiven' (Luke 5:20). This word of forgiveness unlocks a body racked by guilt and frees the man into healing. Faith is a prerequisite for releasing the grace of healing in people's lives. Faith receives the kingdom – for healing is a firstfruit of the kingdom of God, where sickness will be healed and death conquered. 'Do not be afraid, little flock, for your Father has been pleased to give you the kingdom' (Luke 12:32).

Aspects of healing

At Oak Hill Theological College I remember praying with a small group for some close friends of mine called Ray and Nicola Speck, who had been married for a few years. Nicola had suffered from anorexia when she was younger, which jeopardized her chances of having children. On Christmas Eve 1966 she had a stillborn child. A small group of us prayed over her sometime after that, and shortly afterwards she conceived and had a healthy son called Jonathan, who was born in January 1968. Over the following years Ray and Nicola had two further children.

I became Jonathan Speck's godfather, and he was later involved in a remarkable healing. An old lady called Auntie Lottie was at the vicarage having tea. She was wearing a support collar due to the deterioration of her spine. The six-year-old Jonathan had the following conversation with her.

'Auntie Lottie, why do you have a big collar on?'

Lottie told him that she had spinal trouble and needed to wear it to support her neck.

Jonathan then asked, 'Haven't you asked Jesus to make your spine better?'

'No,' Lottie replied, 'I suppose I haven't.'

'Well, don't you think we should?' said Jonathan.

Lottie agreed, and the whole family prayed for God to heal her spine and neck. The next morning Lottie went to the GP feeling much better, and the GP sent her to the hospital to see the consultant. They took X-rays that showed a remarkable healing. Lottie lived for another 25 years, until the age of 98. God answers the natural faith of a little child.

I also remember praying for a friend called Joy who was nearing 40 and had longed for children. I woke one night with a burden for her on my heart, and distinctly sensed God bringing to my mind the story of Hannah in 1 Samuel 1. The next day I had a phone call from a lay reader at St Stephen's, who said he wanted to talk to me about Joy. I said I thought I knew what it was about, and mentioned the birth of a child. He explained that he had dreamed about Joy with a child in her arms. Our two experiences confirmed the messages that we had individually received, and we told Joy. Shortly afterwards she found she was pregnant, and later gave birth to a daughter.

The ministry of healing has always been part of my perspective on ministry and, like many others, I have seen some significant healings but not as many as I would have hoped. I have also experienced occasions when healing does not come in this life, but in a healed death. I have also seen God particularly touch and restore people through crisis times.

One night I was called to Wycombe Hospital when a lady called Ann Bush, whom I knew from a local church, was dying of what they had diagnosed as legionnaires' disease. I went in to pray for her with the laying on of hands. Her husband was with her, and he had been told that she would not live through the night as her liver was failing. I anointed her, prayed over her quietly in tongues, and then left. I did not find out the whole story until some years later, when Ann was ordained and sent me an article from the Oxford diocesan newspaper *The Door*, in which she explained what had happened that night.

> The Hospital Chaplain was called and John Hughes, the former Vicar of St Andrew's High Wycombe, was on duty. I knew him and he just laid hands on me and very quietly and briefly prayed over me. It was like an electric current going through me. An hour before he came to pray my liver was failing but they did another liver function test a little while after he had gone and they could not believe it was normal. I remember there was a young lady houseman standing beside my bed, with a pocket Bible in her white coat pocket, and in response to the doctor's 'It's incredible', she said: 'It's not incredible. It's a miracle.'[6]

This news amazed me. We will often never know the answer to our prayers.

The ripple effect

On another occasion, a member of our congregation at High Wycombe called Albina was involved in a car accident and had a serious whiplash injury. She had treatment at the hospital and went up to Harley Street

---

6 *The Door*, October 1993, p. 6.

for a consultation and diagnosis. They were also trying to decide on compensation. One Saturday that February, we had arranged a healing seminar at the church. I invited Albina to come so that we could pray with her, but she said she had another Harley Street appointment that day. When the day came there was heavy snow, but Revd Margaret Knight from Chorleywood managed to make it through. Albina, however, could not get to London because the trains were cancelled, so she came to the meeting after all.

At the meeting, Margaret gave some clear teaching on prayer and then we prayed for various people. Margaret and I prayed for Albina, who began shaking like a pneumatic drill. This went on for a considerable time. It looked odd, but Albina felt a noticeable decrease in pain. She came to church the next day and said that she had slept without any pain. She was also free in her neck movements and was able to raise her arms without any discomfort.

She had no further trouble, and was discharged from treatment after X-rays showed her so much better. What was remarkable was the consequence of this healing on her husband Abraham, who had lost any faith he had as a young person in the West Indies. Abraham came to church for the first time on Easter Day to hear Albina give her testimony of healing as an illustration of resurrection power. Abraham, who had brought their two sons, was visibly moved.

The next morning Annie had a phone call from Albina, who said that Abraham had had a revelation. 'Tell John,' she said. I went round to see them and discovered that Abraham had taken Albina home from the previous evening's service in a considerable state of agitation. He told her he was deeply troubled and could not settle. They went upstairs to the bedroom and Abraham began to cry out to God. God gave Abraham a revelation of his sin and he remained under conviction, crying out with tears to God for mercy until 4.15 the next morning. Then he came to peace and knew that Jesus had forgiven him.

Abraham's conversion brought about a transformation of his life. God told him he was keeping the wrong company and he broke away from it. He retired shortly afterwards and became our church verger. He turned into a man of such joy and prayer, and the constant prayer on his lips was 'Lord, have mercy'. Abraham and Albina became a much valued couple in the church. God's purpose in healing Albina was much bigger than we had at first thought – his purpose was to bring that family into the kingdom and use them to bless many others in a significant way.

Emotional healings

Much of the emotional and psychological healing I have seen has been concerned with release from the effects of damage and abuse in childhood. I remember a young lady called Yvonne who had been talking and praying with Margaret Hopkinson. Yvonne had come for prayer after one of the services, and her problem was sleeplessness and nightmares. The nightmares always woke her up in torment. Margaret said she thought it was necessary for me to see Yvonne too, and the three of us arranged to meet in the church. Yvonne told us that she had been sexually abused by her father from the ages of 8 to 12 and again from 14 to 16. She had dreaded going to bed and hearing her father's footsteps as he came to molest her. Once she had tried to tell her mother, but she would not believe Yvonne's story, and her father denied it.

I suggested that Yvonne write a letter to God in which she could pour out her feelings about all that had happened. When we met again, she felt this process had been helpful and said she had felt a lot of pain and anger towards both her parents. We used this as a way of praying for her, asking her to tell God how it had been for her and to put her pain into his hands. We also explained that we would ask God to deal with her father, for vengeance is his alone. She was able to give this load to God and let it go. We prayed for God to heal her from the shame and uncleanness that she felt, and to heal both the child and the adult. Yvonne said she felt considerably lighter, and we asked her to let us know how she progressed. She rang Margaret the next morning to say that she had slept well and had no nightmares, so she was very pleased. The next Sunday, however, she said there was something that still troubled her.

We listened and prayed, and I felt the Spirit prompting me to ask if she had ever had an abortion. She said 'yes', and seemed very relieved that it had come out into the open. She had become pregnant at the age of 16 and her father had insisted she should have an abortion. She had felt great guilt and shame ever since, and had never been able to speak about it to anyone. We prayed over this and put the little baby into God's hands. I shared the scripture from Luke, 'He is not the God of the dead, but of the living, for to him all are alive' (Luke 20:38). Yvonne confessed to God her shame and guilt; I absolved her in Jesus' name, and we prayed for healing of mind, body and spirit. This completely released Yvonne, and she has not been troubled further. Some years later she met and married a young man from the church.

Deliverance and spiritual warfare

The other main arena of the healing ministry is the deliverance ministry, or the driving out of evil spirits, so vividly illustrated in the Gospels and Acts of the Apostles. The New Testament view of such matters, despite being so much at odds with that of modern Western society, should be considered without prejudice. Walter Wink comments, 'Angels, spirits, principalities, powers, gods, Satan – these, along with all other spiritual realities, are the unmentionables of our culture. The dominant materialistic worldview has absolutely no place for them.'[7]

Wink sees materialism as terminally ill and seeks to replace it with a worldview capable of honouring the lasting values of modern science without succumbing to its reductionism. He tries to understand the language of powers in the Bible and to interpret this as 'the inner and outer aspects' of any given manifestation of power. The inner aspect refers to the spirituality of the institutions, the 'within' of corporate structures and systems, the inner essence of outer organizations of power. The outer aspect refers to political systems, appointed officials, the leaders of organizations – in short, all the tangible manifestations which power takes. Every power or structure has a 'visible pole' and an 'invisible

---

7 Wink, *Unmasking the Powers*, p. 5.

pole': an outer form, be it a church, a political party, a nation or an economy, and an inner driving force that animates, legitimates and regulates its physical manifestations in the world.

This is a helpful modern way of understanding a biblical worldview that illustrates the way powers can affect and distort individuals and organizations to become destructive rather than wholesome and constructive. When a person or organization becomes idolatrous, placing itself above God's purpose for the good of the whole, then that person or power becomes demonic. The church's task and calling is to recall the powers to their created purpose in the world, so that 'through the church, the manifold wisdom of God should be made known to the rulers and authorities in the heavenly realms'.[8] The powers are capable of redemption, and the church's task is often to bring about that redemption on the basis of faith in the one who has conquered the powers through the cross (see Colossians 2:15).

This perception does not allow a divorce between the material and the spiritual, but holds both together and allows integration for healing. We seek to deal with the whole, both the inner and the outer realm of reality. I have found this model helpful in dealing with the whole area of demonization and evil in its varied forms. The outward manifestations are often projections of an inner disquiet. It is of vital importance to discern and understand what might have led to that disquiet.

Spiritual warfare includes everything that belongs to the battle for the coming kingdom of God and the destruction of the enemy's kingdom. The kingdom of

---

8 Ephesians 3:10.

God is God's dynamic power coming to rule in our lives and in our communities, bringing *shalom*, peace. Waging that battle includes being filled with the Spirit, proclaiming the gospel, making disciples, living a life of praise, prayer, repentance, forgiveness and love, practising healing, acts of mercy and justice, and resisting evil. The Bible gives a picture of the reality of evil as a cosmic battle which affects human lives. Evil has the power and permission that we give it through our sin and wrong choices, or through the sins of others past and present.

Vital principles

When it comes to the deliverance ministry and spiritual warfare, there are three vital underlying principles. First, this is Christ's ministry. He gives his authority to his disciples to carry it out (Luke 9:1; Mark 16:17). Second, such ministry is done in his name. It is in response to his name that evil spirits go (Acts 16:18; 19:13ff.). Third, the ministry stems from the victory of Christ over Satan on the cross. We are not fighting for a victory, but from a victory (Colossians 2:14–15; Romans 8:37–39; 2 Corinthians 10:3–5; Revelation 20:10).

Dangers

There are also some dangers and difficulties to be aware of. The first is the danger of spiritual pride, particularly if we forget the three principles given above, or if we embark on the ministry alone or without the prayer backing of others. It is interesting to note in Ephesians, where Paul speaks much of spiritual warfare, that he reflects two important features. One of these is the sense of the corporate – the 'you' is plural. The major protection for those practising this ministry comes from the body functioning as one. The other feature is the importance of living a holy life: the best weapon of spiritual warfare is the right lifestyle.

Thus Paul's primary call in Ephesians is about 'holy living', following our recognition of being made alive in Christ (Ephesians 2). He goes on to speak about the church and God's plan to make known through the church his manifold wisdom (Ephesians 3:10). Then he speaks of unity as the prize to keep, and of living a life worthy of the gospel by putting off falsehood, anger and deceitful talk, and growing up into Christ. He then speaks of loving relationships in the family, between husband and wife, children and parents, and between colleagues in the workplace.

Spiritual warfare is a battle against the enemy's attempt to bring distortion into God's purpose for creation. It is not simply defensive, but involves living a positive lifestyle in the power of the Spirit. It means living a lifestyle that is opposite to the culture of the world. The way we live our lives is an act of spiritual warfare.

A second danger is the rejection of reason. Like worship, the deliverance ministry should be conducted in the Spirit and in truth. We should watch and pray. Careful observation and skilful diagnosis are vital (Mark 9:21). Spiritual gifts such as discernment are checked and balanced by reason (1 Corinthians 12:10; 14:32).

Third, we must reject any idea of a dualism that positions the demonic as an equal and opposite force to the divine. Unhealthy preoccupation with the demonic and forces of evil can lead to the idea that there is a battle going on between two equal forces. The truth is that the victory already belongs to Christ (Hebrews 2:14).

Fourth, we must beware of modern scientific reductionism, which seeks to explain away what is not scientifically provable. An equal error is to believe that every manifestation must be demonic. Such an attitude denies moral choice and personal responsibility.

A helpful picture showing evil as a distortion has been shared among a team of advisers on healing and deliverance in the Birmingham diocese. It is called the

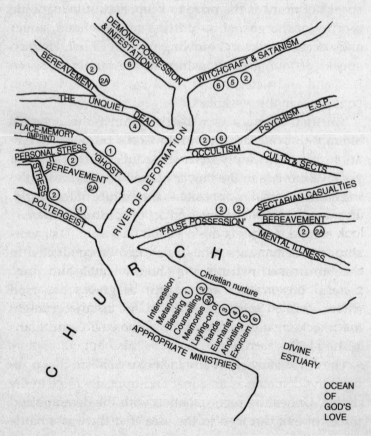

'River of Deformation', for all such activity is a deformation of what God originally intended. The picture illustrates the ocean of God's love and the church's ministries for the growth of life and godliness. These include the ministries appropriate to the different levels of disquiet that evil brings, and the means by which the church can minister wholeness and healing to bring about reformation. The river has a number of tributaries flowing from it, which speak of different levels of oppression that lead to greater destruction and deformation. It also indicates the great need for doctors, psychiatrists, psychologists, nurses, counsellors and clergy to be working in tandem and dealing with the whole person, rather than working only in their separate disciplines.

People and places

Most of the pastoral cases we deal with are ultimately to do with people, but occasionally they will also affect places. We will sometimes be called in to deal with poltergeist activity. This is nearly always associated with unreleased psychic or mental tension. It is important to look for severe emotional stress, marital tension, business worries, blackmail, etc. The truth will take care and time to discover, and will generally lead to counselling and prayer, not exorcism. There can also be 'place memories', where repeated actions took place, for instance a stage-coach entering a yard. The fabric of the environment acts as a sort of screen which projects this happening, and some very sensitive people are able to see it.[9]

---

9 For more on this fascinating subject, please see *The Reluctant Exorcist* by Ken Gardiner (Kingsway, 2002).

Sometimes there is evidence to suggest that earth-bound spirits may be left in a house – suggesting that after death some people (or perhaps the demons that afflicted them) 'hang around' a place or family where their treasure was. Jesus said that people who focused their treasure on earth would be bound to it. Sometimes they have not been able to let go. Often it will be helpful to pray for that letting go and for peace, so that the person may move on. The *Common Worship* funeral service has a wonderful commendation:

Go forth from this world:
In the love of God the Father who created you,
In the mercy of Jesus Christ who redeemed you,
In the power of the Holy Spirit who strengthens you.[10]

This declares an ending of the earthly life in order that the soul may move on in its journey, and importantly the declaration is made to all who are assembled at the funeral service.

There is also some evidence that spiritualists can project an image in order to cause fear or to guard a sacred site. This might happen where animal or human sacrifice has taken place. It is important to be well prepared and to work as a team, and to know how such access was gained. Such activity will cause a spiritual block, either to a building or to a piece of land. Sometimes this can cause a demonic infestation which blocks or hinders the life of the Spirit.

Russ Parker speaks of the intimate connection between land and people. The murder of Abel by Cain,

10 *Common Worship*, Funeral Service, p. 376.

for example, clearly affected the land. God confronted Abel with his action, saying,

> What have you done? Listen! Your brother's blood cries out to me from the ground. Now you are under a curse and driven from the ground, which opened its mouth to receive your brother's blood from your hand. (Genesis 4:10–11)

Russ says, 'Here is the listening God who knows the stories attached to places and challenges the living to take note of them also.'[11] The story intimates that God has in mind to heal wounded people and the land affected by their actions. The effect of Cain's sin was to bring dysfunction to the land and to the people involved. The gospel is one of redemption. Part of the purpose of the coming kingdom is to usher in the first-fruits of that redemption, so that we might be connected, rooted and able to grow in relationship both to people and to the land.

I remember being asked by a vicar to come to his church, where he had recently discovered a trauma that had taken place some years back. During an interregnum a churchwarden had given permission for the church to be used by a group of people for a service. He did not know that the group used it for a black mass and that a young girl provided a foetus for this mass. Some years later, that woman became a Christian and her story came out in the counselling that followed. The vicar and a team gathered to pray with the woman. They prayed at certain places in the church, using holy

---

11 Russ Parker, *Healing Wounded History* (Darton, Longman & Todd, 2001) p. 9.

water for cleansing and restoration.[12] One encouraging result of this was that new people came to the church and became Christians, which had not happened for some time.

Such activity affects people as well as places. Mental illness can, however, mimic demon possession in many cases, and good sense and discernment are necessary. Depressive psychosis, schizophrenia or organic psychosis, which can be induced by drugs, alcohol, glue-sniffing, a brain tumour or epilepsy, all require medical help, loving support and counselling. We may also meet a condition called hysterical pseudo-psychosis. Sufferers of this are very prone to suggestion, and any idea that there may be some demonic element influencing them can trigger off the appropriate reaction. Professional help is needed here.

Confession and responsibility

I often find that in ministering to those who have been oppressed or demonized, I return to the baptismal confession, for in those promises we are turning from one kingdom to another. The baptismal confession identifies us with Christ and his victory on the cross over sin and the powers of evil. In that confession we turn to Christ who is the light and King over all. We repent of our sins, and of anything we may have done to open the door for darkness or evil to invade either persons or places. We renounce the evil one and the works associated with his

---

12 Holy water is water set apart by prayer and dedicated for use in baptism or deliverance. It symbolizes our incorporation into Christ and his loosing us from the powers of darkness.

kingdom. Sometimes we may do this because we have opened that door by turning to the powers of darkness, or it may be that in our family others have opened this door in the past. The gift of repentance and renunciation is a key to unlocking that past and moving out of it.

We can never take such a step for others, for we must each take responsibility for ourselves. This is a vital point. If we do not choose for ourselves, we will not move on at all. I can remember ministering for some time to people who were oppressed, but who simply did not want to take responsibility or make choices for themselves. They were asking me to do the praying and to 'make the magic work', but were not themselves choosing to forgive, repent and renounce wrong choices. People who are not willing to take responsibility are not ready for the journey to freedom, or wish to remain in a victim status where others will take responsibility for them. Sometimes they will need time to face up to the reality, but it is wrong to try to do things for them because they will become dependent on you and not move forward in their own lives.

Jesus indicated the importance of this by asking people what they wanted him to do, and that required a choice on their part. For example, he asked the blind man, 'What do you want me to do for you?' The question put the responsibility back in the blind man's court and elicited the faith that was in him for healing. Jesus' next words involved a command requiring an action of response: 'Go . . . your faith has healed you.' Immediately the man received his sight, and he 'followed Jesus along the road' (Matthew 20:32; Mark 10:52; Luke 18:41). The phrase 'followed Jesus along the road' is significant because wholeness and healing will not come simply through ministry but through being part of the body of Christ, connected in loving relationships with other Christians and participating in the sacramental life of the church.

Taking appropriate action

Where there is no obvious mental illness, the scale of evil influence ranges through temptation, sin, habitual sin, compulsions, oppression, bondage, attack and possession. Our ministry should be appropriate to the position on the scale of demonization: it is wisest to match temptation with reassurance, sin with confession and forgiveness, habitual sin with teaching about the power of Christ to overcome. It is best not to mention possession at all, as this can leave the person with a greater disquiet than he or she is already experiencing.

Sometimes, as I intimated earlier, we inherit the sins of the fathers, and this can complicate our ability to follow Jesus unfettered. I remember one man who became a Christian but lived a very promiscuous life. This seemed habitual to him, and though he had much prayer he was constantly overcome by this temptation. When he was being counselled, enquiry was made into his family history. His father had a similar problem, and when the man investigated further, he discovered that his grandfather had run a brothel in the north. Thus this weakness had an ongoing hold on his family. The man prayed with repentance for the sins of his father and his father's father, and renounced the power that had held them over the years. A group of people prayed for absolution, to cut him off from those past sins by the power of the cross, and for healing, to bring his mind, body and imagination to Jesus for cleansing and renewal. The man found a new freedom to walk in holiness and began to discover a new purity in his thinking especially. He learned to renew his mind, bringing every thought captive to the obedience of Christ.

I want to tell a story of deliverance that involves sexual abuse of a child and the serious ongoing effects that have been traumatic in that child's later life. The story involves a middle-aged lady called Maggie, who was seriously abused by her father without the knowledge of her mother. She was threatened with dire physical consequences if she told anyone. Those threats involved putting a candle near her nightie, saying it would be lit if she told anyone, and wheeling her round a park in a wheelchair saying she would never walk again if she told anyone. Added to this she had an abusive marriage to an alcoholic who abused, beat and tormented her. It does seem that when a child is abused they seem to attract abuse from others as if there was an aura about them that could be picked up.

Maggie had talked and prayed with a chaplain and suffered nightmares, which required medication. Often she woke early with nightmares, which greatly frightened her. I was asked to accompany a health professional who had talked and prayed with her and suggested the visit of a priest, with the permission of the GPs and the psychiatrist. She referred to these nightmares as demons that needed clearing out.

I accompanied this health care worker, listened to Maggie's story and realized the anguish and torment that she had been through for so many years. She was counting on us to bring relief from this torment. She said she had tried to forgive these people. I told her I

wanted to take a Communion service, which declared
that Jesus had triumphed over all the powers of darkness at the cross (Colossians 2:15). I wanted also to ask
her to renew her baptismal vows –

Do you turn to Christ?	I turn to Christ.
Do you repent of your sins?	I repent of my sins.
Do you renounce evil?	I renounce evil.

This she did and I then sprinkled holy water over her –
symbolizing the waters of baptism by which she was
incorporated by faith into Christ. I prayed a prayer com-
manding any spirit to leave her, never to return. Then
we celebrated the Eucharist and prayed over her for
healing, blessing her in God's name. She did not feel
anything happen but said, 'I was touched by a man who
did me no harm.'

Two days later she rang the health professional to say
she had slept soundly that night and the fear had gone.
She felt such relief and had been the next morning to tell
her psychiatrist, whom she was due to see. She
explained to him what had happened. He replied, 'You
don't have to tell me – I can see it in your eyes.'

Ground rules

There are important ground rules to observe when it
comes to prayer for freedom from oppression or for
deliverance. One should never conduct such prayer
alone with the sufferer, for this builds dependency and
risks manipulation and deception, without the wisdom
and counsel of a prayer partner. Jesus sent his disciples
out to pray and minister in pairs, and there is great wis-

dom in that direction. It makes it possible to discuss the way ahead and agree on the best course of action.

In the Anglican Church we minister under the bishop's authorization, so if you are involved in something heavy or that has a deep hold it is wise to refer the case to the bishop or one of his appointed officers and explain what action you are proposing to take. This will prevent some off-the-wall ministry, which can only bring discredit upon the church. Most dioceses have clergy with some experience in this field, who are authorized by the bishop to advise clergy on appropriate action, or who will come in and help directly. Similar reference to professional specialists is common in the National Health Service, where GPs refer cases to consultants so that the best treatment can be given. It is also good to learn from one another in ministry, so that any advice given is not a matter of constraint and restriction, but a matter of sharing wisdom in order to help decide what the appropriate ministry might be in that particular situation.

I recognize how important it has been for me to receive input and encouragement from other ministers who are involved in seeking to advance the ministry of healing and wholeness in a parish situation. It is a vital source of encouragement to be able to share together, discuss obstacles and problems, and to read books written by other practitioners of this ministry. I have been immensely encouraged and built up through my participation in conferences organized by various churches or sponsored by Anglican Renewal Ministries or New Wine. Such gatherings have helped me to persevere in this difficult ministry, and I have learnt a great deal from the teaching of such people as John Wimber, Francis

McNutt, John Richards, Katherine Kuhlman, Russ Parker and Michael Mitton.[13]

Meeting with peers more locally for encouragement and sharing has also been significant in promoting practical ways of growing in the ministry of healing and deliverance. New Wine have organized a network covering the UK in regions, so that leaders can meet together to share experiences and encourage one another in the ongoing practice of ministry. This has been supplemented by a national leaders' conference and New Wine conferences in the summer. It is a vital means of fanning into flame the ministry of healing.

13 John Wimber was the late leader of the Vineyard Movement, and author of several seminal books including *The Power to Heal*. Francis McNutt was a Dominican priest whose books include *Healing, The Power to Heal* and *Deliverance from Evil Spirits*. John Richards is the author of *But Deliver Us From Evil*. Katherine Kuhlman was a remarkable American healer and preacher from the 1950s to the 1980s. Russ Parker is director of the Acorn Healing Trust. Michael Mitton is assistant director of the Acorn Healing Trust and ex-director of Anglican Renewal Ministries.

11

The Image of the Shepherd in the Bible

My concluding chapter explores the image of the shepherd from the biblical tradition. The image of the shepherd and the flock is one of the most meaningful pictures of God's relationship with his people in the Bible, and it spoke powerfully to a herdsman people. I have just spent a week in the Yorkshire Dales, where the images of sheep and shepherd are very familiar. It was lambing time, so the fields abounded with new life, the lambs happily grazing near their mothers. Jesus took this shepherding image as a description of his ministry and mission. Already rich in meaning and symbolism from the scriptures of the Old Testament, the image described vividly the caring, compassionate and arduous nature of sacrificial ministry on behalf of the people God loved.

Origins

In its origins, 'shepherd' or 'herdsman' was an Indo-European word frequently used to describe a leader, ruler or commander. Plato used it when he compared the 'rulers of the city-state' to 'shepherds' who care for the flock. The human shepherd is a copy of the divine shepherd and lawgiver. In the ancient East, 'shepherd' became a title of honour applied to divinities and rulers alike. Before Israel settled in Canaan, the individual tribes travelled constantly with their flocks and herds in search of pasture. The patriarchs were herdsmen, owning sheep, goats and cattle, leading a nomadic existence.

The shepherd's task was undertaken by members of the family, or by daughters in the immediate vicinity of the dwelling. The life of a shepherd was an arduous one, needing to show care, patience and determination to find new pasture at the right time, ensuring a proper balance between grazing, watering, rest and travel. There are no pastures in Palestine, as we understand them. Throughout the East grass is never sown and cultivated, and is not made into hay. The shepherds feed the sheep with crushed straw. The grazing grounds are either the common, unenclosed arable lands round the village, at such time as they lie fallow, or the deserts that occur in and around these lands. These are not the strict pastures of the Bible lands; they consist of lonely, unfenced, uncultivated desert hills and plains where no dwelling is to be seen, save the low black tents of the Bedouin. These are no mere wild wastes, being covered in spring with a glorious wild growth during February to April. The shepherd also protected the flock from harm, guarding the flock at night from thieves and wild beasts, even risking his own life to ensure their safety (see 1 Samuel 17:34–37). He had a shepherd's crook and a rod, or *shevet*, a formidable oak club hung round his neck and used for beating off wild animals.

'Shepherd' in the Old Testament

Micah uses the shepherd image when he calls on Jehovah to come to the deliverance of his people: 'Shepherd your people with your staff, the flock of your inheritance' (Micah 7:14). The story of the Old Testament pictures Yahweh as the only shepherd of his people, Israel. In the Psalter and the Exilic Prophets[1] the idea of the shepherd comes into greater prominence (see Psalm 23; 28:9; 78:52; 80:1; 95:7; 121:4; Isaiah 40:11; Jeremiah 23:2–4; 31:9–10; Ezekiel 34:11–16).

The expression of Yahweh as the 'shepherd of his people' grew out of a living experience of God caring for his people, leading, guiding and providing for them. Through every experience of life, failure, temptation, despair and guilt, and in worship and praise, God's people knew they were still in the hands of God, their faithful shepherd. Israel knew God as sovereign over all, but also as a loving father who cared and provided for his children. The image of the shepherd was a very powerful and comforting allegory for describing God's relationship with his people.

As God's chosen people, Israel is God's flock, possessing a unique and special relationship with God (see Jeremiah 13:17; Isaiah 40:11; Ezekiel 34:31; Micah 7:14; Zechariah 10:3; Psalm 79:13; 95:7; 100:3). When their leaders fail to shepherd their people, God promises that he will raise up a faithful shepherd (David), and that he himself will be their true shepherd.

---

1 *Dictionary of New Testament Theology* Vol. 3 (Paternoster Press, 1978), p. 565.

I am against the shepherds and will hold them accountable for my flock . . . I myself will search for my sheep and look after them . . . I will search for the lost and bring back the strays. I will bind up the injured and strengthen the weak, but the sleek and the strong I will destroy. I will shepherd the flock with justice. (Ezekiel 34:10, 11, 16)

This passage highlights the nature of the Good Shepherd's care for his flock: it involves nurture and care, rescue and healing, strengthening, gathering and protection. These are not just pastoral concerns; there is also a missionary focus that will be a sign to the nations that God is Lord over his people and they are under his care. 'Then they will know that I, the LORD their God, am with them and that they, the house of Israel, are my people, declares the Sovereign LORD' (Ezekiel 34:30).

The shepherd who comes and dies reveals to Israel the nature of God, their true Shepherd, who loves them unconditionally and reveals that love in all his actions. The highest picture of this relationship comes in Psalm 23, where David describes the Lord as his Shepherd and illustrates the nature of his character and activity. No experience of life is excluded from the Shepherd's care and attention. This psalm speaks of his activity on behalf of his sheep, his people. Jesus draws on that image in John 10 when he speaks of himself as the 'good shepherd'.

Kings did not carry the official title of 'shepherd', though they carried that function. Only David is referred to as a faithful shepherd of his people (Ezekiel 34:23–24). The prophets castigate many of the kings for their failure to care for the people because of their arrogance, their disobedience to their divine obligations, and their self-interest.

The Messiah figure that grows out of Israel's need of guidance and care is spoken of as a shepherd sent from God. The prophecies point to a single shepherd (see Jeremiah 3:15; 23:4; Ezekiel 34:23; 37:24). The righteous shepherd is seen as a descendant of David or a messianic figure. Such a figure was particularly emphasized after the Exile in Babylon.

> 'Awake, O sword, against my shepherd,
> against the man who is close to me!'
> declares the LORD Almighty.
> 'Strike the shepherd,
> and the sheep will be scattered,
> and I will turn my hand
> against the little ones.' (Zechariah 13:7)

Most commentaries link this passage with Zechariah 12:10, where the prophet announces a representative death as the preliminary to a dawning of salvation:

> And I will pour out on the house of David and the inhabitants of Jerusalem a spirit of grace and supplication. They will look on me, the one they have pierced, and they will mourn for him . . . as one grieves for a firstborn son.

Thus at the end of the Old Testament shepherd sayings there is an image of the shepherd who suffers death according to God's will and who thereby brings a decisive turn in the history of humankind.

Later Judaism drew distinctions between shepherds. After the Exile the image of shepherds was radically devalued. Shepherds were regarded as poor and often dishonest. The pious were forbidden to buy wool, meat or milk from shepherds. There is a quote in the Midrash on Psalm 23 that 'No position in the world is as despised as that of the shepherd.'

'Shepherd' in the New Testament

The word 'shepherd' occurs nine times in the Synoptic Gospels, six times in John and once each in Hebrews, 1 Peter and Ephesians.[2] The negative view of shepherds was not taken over into the New Testament. Jesus paints a picture of the shepherd's devotion to duty, and uses the metaphor to highlight God's love for sinners and to reveal his opposition to the Pharisees' harsh attitude to the poor. It is particularly to leaders that Jesus' most stinging words are directed (see Luke 11:37–52).

In the Synoptic Gospels Jesus is the messianic Shepherd promised in the Old Testament. They claim that promise for Jesus in three ways.

First, Jesus begins to fulfil the messianic Shepherd's function by gathering together the lost sheep of the house of Israel. 'When he saw the crowds, he had compassion on them, because they were harassed and helpless, like sheep without a shepherd.'[3] This marks the dawn of the era of salvation announced by the prophets. It is this Shepherd who, in compassion, gathers together the shepherdless flock. Yet his mission is not simply for Israel, but for the whole world – 'the power of God for the salvation of everyone

---

2 *Dictionary of New Testament Theology* Vol. 3, p. 566.
3 *Ibid.*

who believes: first for the Jew, then for the Gentile'
(Romans 1:16).

> He will stand and shepherd his flock
> in the strength of the LORD,
> in the majesty of the name of the LORD his God.
> And they will live securely, for then his greatness
> will reach to the ends of the earth.
> And he will be their peace. (Micah 5:4–5)

Second, Jesus will die for his flock and then rise again.
'Jesus told them . . . it is written: "I will strike the shepherd, and the sheep of the flock will be scattered." But
after I have risen, I will go ahead of you into Galilee'
(Matthew 26:31–32; cf. Zechariah 13:7). In this scripture
he identifies himself as the promised 'good shepherd' of
the Old Testament who willingly 'lays down his life for
the sheep' (John 10:11). This death is the means of bringing sheep into God's fold, and it is not exclusive to Israel.

Third, he ushers in the era of salvation in which the
flock of God is gathered under the Good Shepherd,
reaching its completion on the Judgement Day when all
nations will be gathered before the throne of God and
Jesus will separate the sheep from the goats (Matthew
25:31–46). This will bring an end to world mission. After
Jesus' life, death and resurrection the church has been
commissioned to complete the task of proclaiming the
gospel to all nations.

The Good Shepherd of John 10:1–30 is contrasted with
the thief and the hireling. Unlike the thief, the Shepherd
enters through the door and the sheep know him and
follow him willingly. The relationship between the
Shepherd and the sheep is one of intimacy. The sheep

know his voice and trust him because he risks his life to nurture, care for and protect them, something the hireling cannot do.

As the shepherd is an image of the Lord, so the flock is an image of his people. The risen Christ gathers his flock like a good shepherd. This flock includes the Gentiles. There is a divine 'must' in Jesus' mission: 'I have other sheep that are not of this sheep pen. I must bring them also. They too will listen to my voice, and there shall be one flock and one shepherd' (John 10:16).

Peter sees the image of the shepherd as a test of authentic leadership in the church. Jesus is the Shepherd and overseer of our souls. Christian leaders are exhorted not to rule over the flock as tyrants, but as servants so that they may pass the test when the chief Shepherd appears.

> For you were like sheep going astray, but now you have returned to the Shepherd and Overseer of your souls . . . Be shepherds of God's flock that is under your care, serving as overseers – not because you must, but because you are willing, as God wants you to be. (1 Peter 2:25; 5:2)

Jesus the Master Shepherd

With the mobility of life today and the separation of families, there is a great hunger among young Christians for mentoring and spiritual direction that is energizing and releasing not controlling. There is a crying need in the church for this in order to bring disciples to maturity.

Jesus modelled a shepherd's heart and ministry so clearly to his disciples that Peter called the leaders he was training to model that ministry in their oversight of the flock: 'not lording it over those entrusted to you, but being examples to the flock' (1 Peter 5:3).

Jesus left an indelible mark on Peter's life and this was reflected in the way he mentored leaders in the church. Peter as a young leader had been overconfident and brash about his abilities, yet now nearing the end of his journey he called these young leaders to something he had been journeying towards.

> All of you, clothe yourselves with humility towards one another, because, 'God opposes the proud but gives grace to the humble.' Humble yourselves, therefore, under God's mighty hand, that he may lift you up in due time. (1 Peter 5:5–6)

There are three invaluable ways that Jesus helped Peter grow. First, he gave him the freedom and space to fail. True learning comes from a discovery within, which cannot always be found just through heeding the good advice of others. In Jesus' mentoring of Peter, he provided many opportunities for risktaking that would prove a wonderful learning curve. I think of the occasion when the disciples saw Jesus walking on the water when the boat was buffeted by the winds, and they were terrified it was a ghost. Jesus called out to them, 'Take courage! It is I. Don't be afraid.' Peter instinctively replied, 'Lord, if it's you, tell me to come to you on the water.' 'Come,' he said. Then Peter got out of the boat and walked on the water towards Jesus (Matthew 14:26–30). Peter did something the other disciples never experienced because he was courageous enough to take a risk. Even when he began to sink he cried out to the Lord to save him. Jesus didn't scold him for sinking but encouraged him to believe that he could have kept going if he hadn't doubted.

Second, Jesus chose the right time to address issues when Peter could hear. Not before time but when he was ready. Jesus said to his disciples on one occasion, 'I have much more to say to you, more than you can now bear' (John 16:12). The profoundest self-discovery Peter made was through his three-fold denial of Jesus. Jesus expected it and warned Peter of it: 'You will all fall away on account of me.' Peter replied confidently, 'Even if all fall away, I will not.' But Jesus said, 'Before the cock crows twice, you yourself will disown me three times' (Mark 14:28–30).

Shortly after, Peter's denial left him desolate and broken. How mercifully Jesus conveyed he had expected no other response, for he knew what was in Peter, as well as the nature and intensity of the forthcoming battle that they had to endure. Sometimes leaders can be too quick to correct and thus become controlling of others. I shall never forget John Wimber saying it was important to allow the bush to grow and discover its shape, before cutting it back. John the apostle records the Good Shepherd restoring a broken disciple with such tenderness and dignity in John 21. Note how he addressed the point of failure not to embarrass and shame the disciple, but in order that he might be merciful to himself and to others he was to train and mentor in the future. Three times he asks the question 'Do you love me?' and three times Jesus states his commission that Peter is to 'feed my lambs', 'take care of my sheep' and 'feed my sheep' (John 21:15–17).

Third, Jesus saw Peter with faith and called him to fulfil that calling. Goethe said, 'When we treat a man as he is, we make him worse than he is. When we treat him as if he is already what he potentially could be, we make him what he should be.' Jesus encouraged Peter with the confidence to rise up from failure, learn a new dependence and become a channel to help others on their journey.

> Simon, Simon, Satan has asked to sift you as wheat. But I have prayed for you, Simon, that your faith may not fail. And when you are turned back, strengthen your brothers. (Luke 22:31)

So Jesus mentored Peter on his journey and helped him to achieve his God-given potential, so that what he learned he could invest into other disciples. That ministry included encouragement, forgiveness, challenge, confrontation and faith. The gift of encouragement is incalculable in helping people to fulfil God's destiny for their lives.

I notice also that Jesus facilitated growth and development in the lives of potential disciples and even his enemies. He helped them face truth and so come to terms with their wrong attitudes and judgements. I think of the woman at the well who casually met Jesus but was to find this encounter a life-changing experience. In John 4 Jesus meets this woman who has a container of water. He asks for a drink and begins a discussion about a drink that once tasted will never leave one thirsty. This woman has been drinking from the cup of sexual relationships and remains profoundly dissatisfied. The woman is attracted and says,

> 'Sir, give me this water so that I won't get thirsty and have to keep coming here to draw water.' He told her, 'Go, call

your husband and come back.' 'I have no husband,' she
replied. Jesus said to her, 'You are right when you say you
have no husband. The fact is, you have had five husbands,
and the man you now have is not your husband. What you
have just said is quite true.' (John 4:16–18)

It was as she faced the truth of her situation that she
could move from a falsehood to discover where true
meaning was to be found. So the Shepherd of Israel
helps her to come into that place of truth, that place of
reality that is life-changing.

I also notice how Jesus helped people to open themselves to the truth and change their mindsets. There is
the marvellous story of how the Pharisees and teachers
of the law caught a couple in the act of adultery and
brought the woman (not the man) to Jesus for judgement. John records that they made her stand before the
group and said to Jesus, 'Teacher, this woman was
caught in the act of adultery. In the Law Moses com-
manded us to stone such women. Now what do you
say?' (John 8:5). This was a trap, which Jesus initially
ignored by writing something on the ground. They kept
on questioning him until he answered them, 'If any one
of you is without sin, let him be the first to throw a
stone at her.' In these words, Jesus enabled them to step
back from judgement and show mercy, the very quality
they would love to meet for themselves.

Here is the Master Shepherd's wisdom helping disciples to grow and also discover something of the heart of
God himself that is very attractive and contagious. We
need to discover that wisdom in our pastoral care of
others, but only those who have been willing to subject
themselves to such accountability can gain it.

The shepherd role today

The function of leaders is to care for the spiritual welfare of the flock, to give them the nourishment they need for growth and development, to equip them for the work of mission, and to seek the lost, to restore and integrate them into the fold. This image is at the heart of Jesus' understanding of his God-given role as the 'good shepherd', and it forms the basis of pastoral ministry. It is, however, a much bigger and wider concept than we often realize in our understanding or practice of pastoring. When we think of the role of the pastor in the modern church, we often see it as being confined to maintaining and protecting an organism from dying.

Such an inward-looking attitude is directly opposed to church growth. Bishop John Finney highlights an important point when he describes leadership as not simply pastoring individuals, but also equipping individuals to pastor, so that the leader can give energy to grow the church to its full stature.[4] The image of the shepherd in this case emphasizes more care for the individual's nurture and growth, as against care for the whole flock. At times the care for the individual will be in conflict with the care for the whole flock.

When I went to St Andrew's, High Wycombe, the church had just over a hundred adults and families, and one pastor could know the whole congregation. As the church grew, it was not possible to maintain that intimacy. Others had to be trained to carry out pastoral work, and we had a curate. The growing church needed

4 John Finney, *Understanding Leadership* (Darton, Longman & Todd, 1989), p. 44.

the pastor to make that transition, to equip others to carry out the work of pastoral care, so that the leader had time to reflect and give vision to the whole church, thus making continuous growth possible. Many churches do not grow beyond a certain number because the pastor or the people will not allow that transition to be made.[5]

Often people will say there is no pastoral care in their church, meaning that the vicar has not visited them. Yet they may have been visited by laypeople and received real pastoral care from them. The Church of England model of leadership has been largely pastoral, resulting in an imbalance between pastoral care and mission. In a church that grew considerably in numbers, I had to make that transition and the congregation had to learn to give and receive pastoral care from one another. Without that paradigm shift the church will always be directed inwards, rather than reaching out in mission. Any healthy church, of course, needs to do both. The episcopal model of church is a model where the leader delegates pastoral functions to ensure that he has energy to lead his or her team and be focused on the primary vision of worship, training disciples and evangelism, while still providing for the pastoral needs of the congregation and the community. This is particularly necessary in a large and growing church.

---

5 In *Congregation Models of Church* (March/April 1991), Arlin Routharge says that usually one pastor can effectively care for 120 people and know them by name. The church will plateau at that number unless the pastoral work is delegated to others who have been trained and released to provide that care.

A broader view

Paul's vision of the church had that larger vision of mission and pastoral care in mind. He expresses his breadth of understanding in his teaching in Ephesians 4, where he enlarges on the gifts of Christ to his church. He speaks of the role of the fivefold ministry that is essential to the equipping and building up of the church. Without the fullness of this ministry, the church will always be a distortion of what it should be.

> It was he who gave some to be apostles, some to be prophets, some to be evangelists, and some to be pastors and teachers, to prepare God's people for works of service, so that the body of Christ may be built up until we all reach unity in the faith and in the knowledge of the Son of God and become mature, attaining to the whole measure of the fullness of Christ. (Ephesians 4:11-13)

The church can never reach its full potential without this fivefold ministry being given full expression. In the medieval period the church in Rome was based on a minster model, with a centre reaching out in mission to the region around Rome. Rich benefactors built churches on their land, and the founders acted as patrons. This embryonic model later developed into the parish system that was to cover England, thus providing a means for the faith to be nurtured across the country. While that pastoral structure was valid for a nation that had been Christianized, it is inadequate for a mission context such as the pagan culture which prevails in Britain today. The structuring of the church with bishops, presbyters and deacons has left it equipped for nurture and teaching the faith, but considerably weakened for mission. The church has failed to impact the British people entering the dawn of a postmodern culture because it has been tied to maintenance rather than mission. Its resources have been tied up with buildings and its own members, rather than responding to a new context and reaching out to proclaim the gospel to a new and different generation.

The twentieth-century church largely failed in its responsibility to engage in mission to the nation and in church-planting. Two world wars scarred the soul of the nation in a way that never quite mended, and many lost their faith in those terrible times. Archbishop William Temple attempted to reach out in mission to convert the nation, but this was never followed through, as he died before he could see his vision realized. The signs of a new age dawning in the 1960s, with the students' revolt in Paris in 1968 and the dying of an old culture, were not understood quickly enough and the church lost both respect and influence.

It was only in the 1990s that the Church of England awakened once again to its responsibility for mission, with Archbishop George Carey's call for 'a Decade of Evangelism'. This placed the issue of mission to the nation at the forefront of the churches' agenda. Yet despite the attempts of initiatives such as Springboard and Alpha, which has been a remarkable tool for turning the church outward in mission, the impact has not been extensive. Established churches have been too stuck in the past and have not been awake to the gradual paganizing of our culture. Those who have had most success have been the new, growing churches that have been free to move in new ways without the restraints of history and tradition.

A fivefold structure

The fivefold ministries described in Ephesians provide a structure for equipping and growing the church. The apostles, personally authorized by Jesus, were witnesses of his resurrection. Their ministry was not confined to one place and their authority was recognized through the whole church. They were not limited to the Twelve, for Paul, Barnabas, James, Silvanus, Andronicus and Junias were also recognized as Apostles (see 1 Corinthians 15:7; 1 Thessalonians 2:6; Romans 16:7).[6] An apostle had two qualifications: he must have seen Jesus, and he must have been a witness of the resurrection of Jesus (Acts 1:21–22). While no one fits that bill today, in a physical sense, the notion of being called as a witness of the life and resurrection of Jesus is still necessary for those who would have an apostolic ministry.

The prophets unveiled the will of God to God's people and to national leaders. They had an itinerant ministry and spoke as directed by the Holy Spirit. Their words were to be weighed by those in leadership roles in the church, and various tests of prophecy were given in order to secure that objective (1 John 4:1–4). The role of the prophet was open to abuse, so other tests were also developed in the early church. If a prophet stayed more than three days, for example, then he was considered a false prophet using his office to sponge on people.

The evangelists were also wanderers, bringers of good news. They did not have the kudos of the apostles

---

6 The definition and understanding of 'apostle' is given fuller treatment in *The Apostle's Notebook* by Mike Breen in this series.

or prophets, but they took the gospel to a world that had not heard it. There are examples of evangelists in the Acts of the Apostles (chapters 6–8) among the seven who were made deacons. Philip and Stephen carried out an evangelistic ministry, as bringers of the gospel to new situations.

The role of the pastor and teacher developed as the church became established. They had a permanent role in the oversight of one congregation and were charged with building up the body of Christ to function effectively. Their ministry was supplemented by visits from the apostles and prophets. Timothy and Silas carried out a teaching and pastoral function with Paul, as well as being sent to the churches as leaders at Ephesus and Corinth.

Pastors and teachers ministered in three ways. First, they had a responsibility for transmitting the story of Jesus by word of mouth – they were repositories of the gospel.

Second, they were to teach the faith to others so that they might also teach others. Such mentoring enabled new leaders to develop and helped the church to grow. 'And the things you have heard me say in the presence of many witnesses entrust to reliable men who will also be qualified to teach others' (2 Timothy 2:2).

Third, these teachers were also pastors, or shepherd figures, who were guardians of the flock and responsible for nurturing faith, so that the whole church was involved in the work of ministry. This picture of the shepherd, as we have seen, is an indelible part of the New Testament. Shepherds cared for the flock and led them to safety. They sought the lost sheep and risked their lives to protect them. They bore them on their hearts, fed them with God's truth, and defended them in their faith.

This ministry, however, is much wider in its scope than simple pastoral care. It includes encouragement, admonition and setting relationships in order, confronting what could so easily divide and decimate the church. It challenges self-interest and calls the people of God to rise up and fulfil their God-given commission.

> Go and make disciples of all nations, baptising them in the name of the Father and of the Son and of the Holy Spirit, and teaching them to obey everything I have commanded you. And surely I am with you always, to the very end of the age. (Matthew 28:19–20)

It is in obedience to that journey that the church can be assured of its survival and the continuing presence of Jesus.

Each ministry is exemplified in the person of Jesus. Paul's image of the church is of a community growing to maturity, 'attaining to the whole measure of the fulness of Christ', growing into a lithesome body equipped for all tasks. Christ is the Bridegroom coming for his church. When he comes it will not be for an inferior bride. His bride will be beautiful, whole and mature. She will be responsive to his voice, and without blemish. This is God's vision for the church, which we need to keep ever before us. The Holy Spirit is at work in her to bring her to this place and the fivefold ministries are key to her becoming like Christ.

Other books in the Ministry Guides *series . . .*

The Prophet's Notebook
by Barry Kissell

The first in an exciting new series consisting of five
'Notebooks', each covering a different ministry listed
by Paul in Ephesians 4. *The Prophet's Notebook* will help
prophets to recognise their gifts and use them to build
up the people of God.

The Apostle's Notebook
by Mike Breen

Interest in the apostolic ministry is increasing within
many streams of Christianity. Mike Breen looks at what
the Bible has to say and comes to some surprising and
challenging conclusions on the role of the apostle in
today's church.

The Evangelist's Notebook
by John Peters

If you could look inside the heart and mind of an
evangelist, what might you see? A passion for those
who have yet to discover the love of God in Christ?
But what is an evangelist to make of the church at
a time when so few are being added to it? Can the
inevitable frustration be used in a positive way?

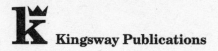

Kingsway Publications

The Teacher's Notebook

by Mark Stibbe

'Evangelists bring people in. Teachers bring people on.'

Mark Stibbe practises what he preaches in this gold-dust guide to the art of teaching and preaching – ideal for anyone who wishes to develop their gift. Learn how to use illustrations that 'touch the heart in order to tease the mind'. Make effective use of questions and pithy sayings as you teach for a life response.

Ideal for both those who teach topically and those who use set Bible readings (including a lectionary) as they seek to interpret and apply the word of God in the power of the Spirit.

'I am always at a banquet when I hear Mark teaching. This book will inspire and equip all teachers of the Bible to be more effective.'

J. John, author and evangelist

'This is Mark Stibbe at his best. Every minister and church leader should read it.'

R. T. Kendall, former Minister of Westminster Chapel, London

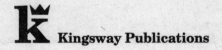 **Kingsway Publications**